A Teenage Girl's Guide To Being Fabulous

Suzanne Virdee

ISBN: 1502491591
ISBN 13: 9781502491596

About the Author

Suzanne Virdee is a journalist. She was ten years old when she decided she wanted to make journalism her career. Growing up, she wrote and produced newspapers for her family, selling them for ten pence each. After leaving school, she set about becoming a reporter, deciding against advice to go to university and get a "proper" job instead!

She spent the summer writing to around ninety local newspapers and radio newsrooms all around the country, asking to be taken on as a junior reporter. Instead of a promising offer, all the post brought was a whole heap of rejection letters. Down but not defeated, she wrote to the *Solihull Times* newspaper in the West Midlands, offering to work for a week for nothing to gain experience. They accepted, and due to another reporter being away ill, she ended up writing the entertainment news page and getting her first byline.

By the end of the week, her fortunes had completely changed. The editor called her into his office and offered her a job as a junior reporter. She was on her way and has never looked back.

She went on to work for the *Sunday Mercury* in Birmingham and the *Birmingham Evening Mail* before switching to broadcast journalism. She worked in BBC and commercial radio newsrooms as a producer, reporter, and presenter before heading to television news. She worked for ITV News before being poached to present the regional news programme *BBC Midlands Today*, a job that saw her win a Best Presenter award. She was also a regular face on *BBC Breakfast News in London*. She is now freelance and lives in Worcestershire with her husband, Andrew Fox, an award-winning photojournalist, and their rescue cat, Monty.

Contents

Introduction

There is no great secret to being a fabulous girl. Being fabulous is not just for the rich and beautiful. It's a state of mind. It's something we can all be. We are all born fabulous. It just sometimes gets knocked out of us as we grow up. A harsh word here or a bad experience there, or just negotiating the growing pains of teenage years, can leave us feeling anything but fabulous sometimes. But another factor is the speed at which growing up happens in the twenty-first century. As girls, there is so much pressure to be sexy, to dress sexily, to "sext," and to have sex at a younger and younger age.

Social media is a brilliant tool, but it brings a darker side too that can be difficult to get your head around. It brings instant access to a full-on, adult world of porn, a world of "trolling" and "sexting," a world of hundreds of Facebook friends you have never even met and can never know. It can be overwhelming.

Once, bullies were only encountered in the playground. Now, "trolls" can get you twenty-four hours a day, even in the safety of your own home!

That's a heck of a lot for us adults to deal with, but for young people just learning about life, it can bring a whole heap of questions, stress, and worries. It can normalise and distort behaviour that face-to-face would not be normal or acceptable at all. On top of this, there are the small matters of schoolwork and exams and working out what you want to do with your life.

None of this would be so hard to deal with if there were rules on how to handle it, but there is no rule book. What you do is up to you. That is great. It is freedom. But how do you use that freedom if you don't understand what's happening around you? To make good decisions, we need to know all the facts, and that's what this book is about. It's about helping you to be your fabulous true self. We all mature at different speeds. We all have different views on things. What I want for you is not to be afraid or confused and to be wise to the world around you.

I assumed that by the time we got to the twenty-first century, all girls would expect to be treated equally to boys in all things. After all, we are years on from the old-fashioned idea that a woman's place is to stay at home, bring up children, and cook and clean. I had hoped these outdated ideas had been well and truly buried thanks to previous generations of feminist women who were sick of being treated as second-class citizens and fought back against the system and old fashioned social attitudes. These women protested with banners and direct action. They became known as the "bra burners" although that was mainly mythical. They really got noticed by holding public demonstrations. Feminist magazines were launched. These actions grabbed the headlines and became a symbol of their independence and their determination to be treated fairly and also equally to men. They were very successful. Several laws such as the Equal Pay Act, The Sex Discrimination Act, and The Domestic Violence Act were passed in the 1970s.

The whole idea of empowerment and "girl power" has got a bit muddled over the years. Many girls your age are growing up with some odd views of what it means to be a girl and a woman. This is not your fault. It is society's problem. When I say "society," I mean the shared beliefs, values, and activities of people in general. Instead of turning out a new generation of strong, happy, fearless young women, comfortable in the fact that they are equal in society to men and will be treated fairly, we are in danger of producing generations of young girls unhappy about themselves and their bodies and doubting their ability to achieve while they believe that men are in charge.

Feminism emerged because women wanted equal rights to men. They wanted to have a career. They wanted to be in charge of their own bodies. They wanted to choose if and when to get pregnant. They wanted access to contraception outside marriage. They also fought for equal pay. However, more than forty years after the Equal Pay Act was brought in, it is still not happening.

In fact, according to the Fawcett Society which works to close the equality gap, in 2013 the gender pay gap got bigger for the first time in five years. The pay gap between women and men currently (in 2015) stands at 19.1 per cent.

This pay inequality breaks the law, but no one seems to address it. This sends out the message that women are not worth as much as men in society. It also puts women at a financial disadvantage. Life is expensive. A 19 per cent difference in pay can mean the difference between being able to buy your own home or not. It may mean the difference between affording good-quality food or not. It may mean the difference between having enough to live on when you are old, or not.

When it comes to pay, it is also depressing that women only make up around 12 per cent of high-earning company bosses in this country. Compared to men, many more women get stuck in low-paid and often part-time jobs. Almost two-thirds of people being paid just seven pounds an hour are women *(Source: Fawcett Society. fawcettsociety.org.uk)* Is it because we are less capable than men? No. I think it is down to a few things. One is that women have come to accept the unfairness that exists towards them. Two, they do not think that complaining will make a difference, and three, they can't see how to change it.

The unfairness in pay is also partly down to the fact that it's men who run our companies and make the big decisions in our country. It doesn't affect them, so it is not a critical issue on their agenda. The recent recession has been used as a reason not to put up pay, full stop. It was also used as a reason not to tackle unequal pay between men and women, but even now, after the recession, nothing has changed.

So how can you, as schoolgirls, get a better deal for yourselves? Well, I hope my book will give you food for thought. My job here is not to brainwash you to think one thing or another but to spur you on to decide for yourself what sort of world you want to live in and what you want to achieve and to encourage you to make it happen. My biggest aim is that you start to believe you can change things. I want you to know you can achieve just as much as boys. You could run a big company if you want to, or run the country one day. I want you to know that as a young woman, it is your right to have the same opportunities as men.

I am sad to say that lots of girls nowadays do not believe they are equal to boys. Too many naturally assume boys have the upper hand. That boys are in charge. Why do I say such a thing? Well, it came as a shock when I read these statistics:

One in three schoolgirls believe it is OK sometimes to hit a woman or force her to have sex. One in two boys think this too.

(Source: EVAW, End Violence Against Women; endviolenceagainstwomen.org.uk/preventing-violence-against-women)

I am stunned and very worried by this. Why do so many girls think so little of themselves? What on earth has happened by your tender age to make so many of you think boys are in charge of you and that you should expect to be treated badly by them? Also, why do so many boys believe girls are inferior and that they should be able to control them with violence? If we do not change this, I believe it will affect the kind of boyfriends, husbands, work colleagues, and friends these boys will grow up to be. We will be edging back to a world where women were widely considered second-rate to men.

Women are not physically as strong as men. That's a fact. Women have babies, and men can't. That is it. These are the only differences, and these differences shouldn't be seen as weaknesses or inferiority. Boys are not a superior creation, no matter what they tell you!

A Little Bit about Me

I was born to a white English mother and an Indian father. It was, and is to this day, sadly, seen by many families across India and elsewhere in the world as undesirable to have a baby girl. In China, many baby girls are abandoned. Some are killed before being born, and sometimes shortly after. This is because there is a strict one-baby-per-couple policy, and families often want boy babies who will grow up to be able to work hard physically and support the family. Girls are seen as unable to do hard, physical work. It is widely thought that girls will be incapable of financially looking after elderly relatives when they grow up.

Girls generally, in many countries, are seen as costing money, and therefore they are seen as a burden. Educating them is not seen as important because their destiny is marriage and looking after the family. Those who are lucky enough to go to school often are not allowed to continue their education after puberty, and even if they do, it is unlikely they will be allowed to pursue a career. Marriage is their destination, and for the majority, that often means an arranged marriage or, much worse, being forced to marry someone they don't want to. Shockingly, forced marriage happens in the United Kingdom too, despite it being illegal. If this is something you are worried about or you need help and advice about, you can call **the Forced Marriage Unit on 020 7008 0151 or visit www.gov.uk/forced-marriage.**

Culturally, in India, it is boys who are prized above girls. (*Source: International Center for Research on Women, icrw.org/publications/son-preference-and-daughter-neglect-india*) It is the young men and their families who receive dowries from the girls' families before a wedding. Dowries are usually gifts of money but can also be gifts of jewellery or clothes or even a car. Although dowries are against the law in India and have been since 1961, in reality, it is a tradition that is still expected by many. Families demanding bigger dowries cause around eight thousand women to be killed a year. (*Source: India National Crime Records Bureau*). Dowry extortion puts great financial burden on the bride-to-be's family.

Luckily, my dad was among those forward-thinking men who cherished girls as much as boys. He told me: "You are my son and my daughter, and I love and want the same things for you as I would a son."

Hearing that from a young age and having many strong-minded women in my family, my amazing mother being just one of them, made me strong and able to cope with the ups and downs life brings. It meant that I always believed, without even realising it, that I am just as good as anybody else, boys included! But it also taught me to be fearless and go for what I want in life. As far as I am concerned, this is what all parents, teachers, and society generally should say to all girls from the youngest of ages and keep telling them, and that is what I want to say here to you. **Girls, you are just as good as boys.** They are your equals and not your superiors. There is nothing you cannot achieve if you put your mind to it.

What qualifications do I have for writing this book? Well, I was a girl and am now a woman.

This book is simple, really. This is what life experience and my extraordinary family have taught me, and it has never let me down. If I had a daughter, this is what I would tell her.

one

Sparkle

What do I mean by "sparkle"? Well, it is an energy, a vibrancy around a person, someone who has that extra something. Sparkle is that thing that gets us noticed for the right reasons. It's inside all of us. You may not realise it, but you have it too.

Sparkle is really confidence with a twist. It's about refusing to think you can't do something. It's about getting the most out of your life and not being scared to speak up and voice your opinions. It's about feeling that you are just as good as anyone else. It's also about being able to dream big dreams and believe without doubt that you can achieve them.

> *No one can make you feel inferior without your consent.*
> *—Eleanor Roosevelt (1884–1962), US first lady, diplomat, and human rights activist*

When I say "sparkle," I don't mean wearing sparkly clothes, of course. As much as I love them, it would be a bit weird if someone did that all the time! It also doesn't mean hanging out with a certain crowd or being the most popular girl at school. It means quietly but firmly believing in yourself and not allowing anyone to make you feel inferior. It means feeling that you belong. Feeling you can do anything.

This is not as impossible to achieve as it might sound.

Film stars, pop stars, sports stars, top business people, and political leaders all have "sparkle." People who have achieved great things in life have it in spades! They don't have it as a *result* of what they have achieved. They had it before they hit the big time. They used sparkle to achieve their success. You can too.

Don't get sparkle mixed up with showing off or ego. Those are empty, silly things. It's more than that. Sparkle is genuine. Sparkle is what we all need to carry us through the good and not-so-good times.

When we leave primary school and go to secondary school, life gets more serious. We are faced with learning lots of new subjects in class, making new friends, and mixing with lots of people who are older and "cooler" than us.

Those of you reading this book will come from all sorts of different backgrounds. Some of you will have more money than others, more opportunities, and more support at home than others. Some of you may feel alone or feel you have no one who seems to bother about what you do. You might have parents who expect you to follow a certain path and profession, and that can pile a lot of pressure on you. You may have recently come to this country with your family and be getting used to a whole new culture. Money may be tight and opportunities where you live limited. You may not have a mum. You may not have a dad. In fact, you may not have either. You may be in care or living with other family members. None of that matters, because **it doesn't matter where you come from— it's where you are going that counts.**

Whatever is happening in your world right now won't stay that way forever. You are growing up, and life will change. It can change for the better or for the worse; much of that's up to you. That's where the need for sparkle comes in.

Sit and think for a minute—dream, even. What career or job do you wish you could have when you leave school or university? Then consider: what do you *really* think you will end up doing when you leave school or university? If you have answered the same for both questions, that is brilliant. You are on track. If the two are wildly different, then we have some work to do. What I want you to automatically believe is that your dreams can be the reality if you put your mind to it.

Going to school is a far cry from being out in the adult world of work. You can get by at school without drawing attention to yourself. If you are going to succeed in the world of work, you need to make yourself stand out. Cue the sparkle! Employers say they hate it when candidates in interviews mumble, don't hold eye contact, and just generally have the personality of a dead dog! It's important to start to get yourself ready for the world of work now.

Most of us go through a period of being shy when we are at school. You may be really loud with your friends, but when it comes to addressing the class, making a speech, or just having to talk to adults in situations out of your normal comfort zone, you may get tongue-tied. Being shy can hold you back. Most of the things that make us feel that way are down to fear—fear of what people might think of us. Fear that if we're doing a speech, our words will come out all wrong and we will be laughed at. The best way to deal with this sort of fear is to be prepared.

Preparation Is the Key to Everything

So, before you have an important conversation— with a teacher, say—stop and think through exactly what you want to say and practise it. Think of the best and the worst outcomes of what could happen in your conversation. Then think about what you would say in both cases. Being prepared like this, even though it sounds a bit odd, will give you confidence, and that equals sparkle!

You can take this technique even further. If you have to talk to the class or host an assembly, imagine yourself walking up to the stage or front of the class and see yourself doing your talk or speech. Think of how you will feel. You can help to kill the butterflies and nerves by running through it in your head and thinking about every stage of what you have to do. Take a few really deep breaths and never rush what you are saying. If you are doing a speech or presentation, print it out. Typed words are easier to read than handwriting. Practise it out loud at home. If speaking in front of lots of people still terrifies you, just think of them all on the toilet…or in their undies! Grim, but it will make you laugh, and that will relax you!

Nerves are a waste of time and really hold us back. If you prepare well, practise, and stay focused, you will be fine. If you are focused, you will not have time for nerves because you will be concentrating on what you're going to say. In my job as a TV news presenter, I had to do a lot of public speaking, and trust me—these tips do work, and the more you do it, the easier it gets. You'll get the sparkle in no time.

You will also find your peers and teachers and other adults will be blown away by your confidence. Someone who looks and sounds confident always impresses.

Fear holds you back. Sparkle pushes you forward, and practise makes perfect.

People who achieve great things often say they didn't have any doubts or fear about what they were doing. In other words, they just concentrated on the end result, and those horrible nagging doubts about whether they could do it didn't have time to get inside their heads and wreck their plans.

If you can nail these basic communication skills in school, then when the time comes to go for interviews, you will sparkle!

For many of you reading this, your life will more than likely consist of being at home and at school. You may feel distinctly unsparkly right now. What I want to encourage you to do is to get out of your little world and into the big, wide world.

There is a saying: "You learn from experience." Learning new things makes us more interesting too. It helps shape our personality. So get a part-time job, join an after-school club, volunteer in a charity shop. Open your eyes and experience new things.

If you already do some out-of-school activities, that's great. Think about what you are getting out of them. Are you enjoying them? Are you meeting new people? Are you learning new things? If the answer is no, change them and try something new.

By trying lots of new things, you might find you are really good at something you never even thought of having a go at. That might open up a whole new career path.

> *I felt like it was time to set up my future, so I set a goal. My goal was independence.*
> *—Beyoncé, pop superstar.*

Beyoncé has nailed "sparkle." She is very driven and determined. You can be those things too. She's saying she's taken responsibility for her future. Your future is yours to shape. You don't have to be an international pop superstar. Just set your goal and work towards it. No one else can make your dreams come true for you. That's down to you.

As a teenage girl, it's sometimes difficult to get your voice heard. To really nail sparkle, you need to be taken seriously. So, how do you do that? Well, there are a number of things you can do apart from the things I've mentioned. You could start a school newspaper, or, if your school has the facilities, a radio station. All you need is a few like-minded pupils to join you, and of course your head teacher's permission! If they agree, your teachers can help you set it up. Writing for your fellow pupils can be a great way of discussing a variety of subjects that interest or worry you. It will also make you more articulate, will look good on your CV, and will be a great talking point when you go for interviews.

Don't think you can't do these things. You can. Even as a schoolgirl, your voice can and should be heard.

> *When the whole world is silent, even*
> *one voice becomes powerful.*
> *—Malala Yousafzai*

Malala Yousafzai is a schoolgirl campaigner for girls' right to education. She was shot by the Taliban in Pakistan for defying them and going to school. She is the joint winner of the Nobel Peace Prize for 2014. She is the youngest person ever to receive it.

Malala is an incredible girl. She has dared to speak up for girls' rights at such a young age. You don't have to face the terrible consequences she did, but you too can make your voice heard or speak up for issues you are passionate about.

Why not start a girls' club at your school? Meet once a week and talk about subjects that concern you. Ask female teachers for advice and guidance on how to go about this. Maybe you could even produce some theatre or music around the issues you discuss and perform them for the school. It will be fun. It will make you feel more confident, and as a result, you will feel empowered—and yes, you will get that sparkle I keep talking about.

Setting up a girls' group is a great opportunity to explore issues girls face. Look at subjects like female genital mutilation (FGM) and forced marriage. It may surprise you to know that these things affect girls in the United Kingdom even though they are illegal.

FGM sees a girl's genitals cut away. It's a practise carried out across Africa, the Middle East, and Asia. This, as you can imagine, is a painful procedure, and it leads to long-term health issues for women. It's done to babies and older girls to prevent them from having pleasurable sex and prevent them from being unfaithful to future husbands. It's practised in around twenty-nine countries. It affects sixty-six thousand girls and women in the United Kingdom. For more information about FGM, you can go to the Daughters of Eve website dofeve.org. They are working to raise awareness of FGM and stop it. Or call the NSPCC FGM helpline on 0800 028 3550. It is free, anonymous and they are there 24/7. Or log onto their website nspcc. org.uk. It has a big section on FGM.

And everyone in Britain, whatever their religion or belief, has the right to choose whether to get married or not and decide who they want to marry. But forced marriage is affecting girls aged just twelve and thirteen.The website gov.uk/forced-marriage gives advice about what to do if you (or someone you know) are being forced into marriage.

Sex education and relationship talks are woefully lacking in many schools. As young women, you need to know all the facts. Maybe invite an expert in to answer your questions about sex.

Use your girls' group to inspire you as well. Invite successful women, maybe a sportswoman, doctor, pilot, or anyone with an interesting job to come and talk to you about their careers and how they got there. Hearing real-life stories can really help spur you on.

Meeting and talking to other girls can make you feel so much better about yourself. You realise that what worries you also worries other girls. You can support and find strength from one another, and that's really positive.

Believe You Can

To really nail sparkle, you have to believe in yourself.

Never be afraid to speak up, have an idea, or ask a question.

You gain strength, courage, and confidence by every experience in which you really

*stop to look fear in the face. You must
do the thing you think you cannot do.
—Eleanor Roosevelt*

I have been shocked to find out that self-belief is, for too many teenage girls, nonexistent.

A friend of mine who runs confidence workshops for girls told me that once, she asked a group of teenage girls to each tell her one thing they thought was good about themselves or that they were good at. Not one girl put her hand up. She left it as long as she could, thinking they were just shy, before asking them again. Then came the surprising and depressing answer from one girl, who blurted out: "I'm not good at anything."

It turned out that many of the girls thought the same. They all said they had never been told they were good at anything. In fact, some had been told the opposite—that they were useless and were never going to make anything of themselves. The girls had actually started to believe it. This meant they had given up on life before theirs had even started. No one has the right to tell you that you are useless. You are not. We are all good at something.

You have to believe you are just as good as anyone else. Why? Because you are.

*Some people say I have attitude—maybe I
do…but I think you have to. You have to*

believe in yourself when no one else does—
that makes you a winner right there.
—Venus Williams, US superstar tennis player

Venus Williams has won seven Grand Slam singles tennis titles and counting!

If you don't have this sort of belief in yourself and your abilities, you will not succeed. It doesn't matter if ten other people all think you can do something. If *you* don't believe it, you won't achieve it.

Boys tend to have much more of an "I can" attitude than girls. This may be understandable if you think about the roles men and women have historically been allowed to play.

For years, in this country many women only worked until they married. It was always the men who would go out to work while wives were expected to stay at home with the children. Men saw themselves (and were seen by society) as breadwinners. They never got involved in domestic duties. Around the 1950s this was fairly typical.

Even when women did work outside the home, they would often work part time and earn less than men. The man's career was always seen as important, while his wife's was seen as a hobby.

That attitude is so deeply ingrained in our society that even nowadays it's still a novelty to hear about women breadwinners and about men who stay at home and care for their children. It's still a novelty to see women government ministers, successful women scientists, surgeons, or multimillionaire businesswomen. When we do hear about them, we also often hear about their looks and even how their children might be suffering if they work long hours. No one questions who is looking after a man's children when he works long hours. These are the sort of sexist criticisms that, without us realising it, we have got used to. They can make us less likely to believe in ourselves or try to succeed.

My wish for the new millennium is for all children…to grow up wiser, and stronger and more prosperous for the future than ever before.
—Hillary Clinton, former first lady of the United States and former US secretary of state in the Obama administration

Sexism is around us at all ages. When we are little, we are given baby dolls and toys such as mini vacuum cleaners or cookers to play with, while boys are given footballs, guns, and cars. When you think about how girls can now join the army and how many men are top chefs, it seems ridiculous, really. It also underlines the idea that girls should be homely and put others first, while boys are brought up to be sporty, in charge, and macho.

A woman who is an assertive boss and confident in her work is often described as a "bitch" or "bossy." These are both negative, insulting words. A man who is an assertive boss is seen as "strong" and "decisive." These words are complimentary and positive. These are the double standards that exist for successful men and successful women. While it's important to be aware of this sexism, it's also important to have enough self-belief not to let it affect you.

The government is now encouraging women to choose careers in engineering and science. Great! But there are also two big challenges here. One is to get girls to believe they can do them, and two, to get the rest of society to believe they can too! Listen to Dr Maggie Aderin-Pocock, space scientist and presenter for BBC's *The Sky at Night*:

> **I was put in remedial class, and people assumed I was not going to achieve very much...I did feel written-off. It was like people put me at the back of the class where I couldn't do any harm. It was a bit depressing. But I always had a dream...**

This incredible woman went on to become a space scientist. Her quote proves that just because others doubt you, it does not mean they are right.

She also said:

When I got my first job with the Ministry of Defence there were a few times I walked into a room and someone would say, 'Three coffees, love.' There's the initial shock because people aren't used to seeing black female scientists or engineers. I always tried to show them straight away I was competent and get their respect. That's when colour and gender disappear.

(Source: interview for BBC News England)

So, Dr Aderin-Pocock experienced that lazy, inbuilt sexism too. There was an assumption that she was the tea lady because she was a woman in a "man's" world. She didn't let it put her off her dream. Her talent and determination and resilience won the day.

Girls, Ambition Is Not a Dirty Word!

I am passionate that all girls should educate themselves to the highest level and pursue a career that will bring independence and satisfaction. Even if you decide to put it on hold to raise a family, having qualifications and skills will mean in many cases that you can get back into work more easily when you choose to. It's still not made very easy for women to do that, but it is possible and is now being done by more women than before. Remember that while being a mum, a wife, or a partner, you are still you, a person in your own right.

Girls, we can be our own worst enemies. Even when we are told we are good at something, we tend to rush to brush off the compliment. We get embarrassed. Instead of enjoying the praise, we naturally say things like: "Oh no, I'm not that good, really." We are too modest.

We need to learn to take compliments and sing our own praises more. We need to be proud of what we achieve. Boys tend not to have this problem. They automatically believe in themselves more than girls. That's probably another reason why men go further in their careers than many women. They achieve more because they *believe* they can achieve it. They believe that success or a promotion is their right. What I would like you to remember is that it is your right too.

Society still has lower expectations for women in the workplace than for men, and you have to challenge that.

School is the right time to start to make your mark. Make it clear to your teachers that you have ambition and drive and want to work hard and do well in life. If you're struggling with a subject, ask your teacher for help.

We have to reshape our own percep-
tion of how we view ourselves.
—Beyoncé

If you think about what you want from life, you will probably spend just as much time thinking about how you cannot possibly achieve it! Do not weigh yourself down with thoughts of all the obstacles that *might* come your way or the fact that it may take years to achieve your dream. None of us can be worried about things that *might* happen or we'd never do or achieve anything.

Work hard and do not be scared of achieving.

A great tennis career is something that a
fifteen-year-old normally doesn't have. I hope
my example helps other teens believe they can
accomplish things they never thought possible.
—Maria Sharapova, tennis superstar

Maria Sharapova is a Wimbledon Champion (to name just one of five Grand Slam titles to date)!

Sometimes I think we think, and society tells us, we are too young to achieve things or believe in ourselves. We are told we should wait until we grow up. If you are talented at something, go for it. Achieve while you are young. Don't hold yourself back.

Girls, we are lucky enough to be in a country where, as children, we are all given the same education and start school at the same age. It is up to us what we decide to do with that opportunity. For girls in many other parts of the world, that opportunity doesn't exist. In fact, being a girl is often a burden. The facts below show what a tough life some girls face. I hope reading this will drive you to rise above any obstacles in your life and make you more determined than ever to get yourself a great education.

These are some facts about how a lack of education affects girls around the world. They are even more striking when you realise that women make up half the world's population! These statistics come from a variety of organsations, for more information just pop the source in brackets into Google.

- **Globally, 66 million girls are out of school. (UNESCO)**

- **Eighty per cent of all human trafficking victims are girls. (UNFPA)**

- **There are 33 million fewer girls than boys in primary school. (Global Education First)**

- **Seventy-five per cent of AIDS cases in sub-Saharan Africa—the region hardest** hit by the disease—are women and girls. (UNAIDS)

In a single year, an estimated 150 million girls are victims of sexual violence. (UNIFEM)

- Fifty per cent of all the sexual assaults in the world are on girls under 15. (UNFPA)

- Fourteen million girls under eighteen will be married this year; thirty-eight thousand today; thirteen girls in the last thirty seconds. (UNFPA)

- The number-one cause of death for girls aged fifteen to nineteen is childbirth. (World Health Organisation)

Girls with eight years of education are four times less likely to be married as children. (National Academies Press)

- A child born to a literate mother is 50 per cent more likely to survive past the age of five. (UNESCO)

Educated mothers are more than twice as likely to send their children to school. (UNICEF)

- School is not free in over fifty countries. (UNESCO)

- A girl on planet Earth has a one in four chance of being born into poverty. (The World Bank)

- A girl with an extra year of education can earn 20 per cent more as an adult. (The World Bank)

- If India enrolled just 1 per cent more girls in secondary school, their gross domestic product would rise by around £3.2 billion.

Bear with me here on this last item—the gross domestic product (GDP) is the total value of goods and services produced in a country in a year. In other words, it is the wealth of a country. This proves that girls *are* worth educating. (*Source: CIA World Factbook*) (*Global Campaign for Education and RESULTS Education Fund*)

Going to school and working in jobs they enjoy are dreams that will remain just dreams for millions of those girls. Imagine that, and seize your chance to be the best you can.

I have already mentioned Malala Yousafzai. She is a girl who was born in Pakistan, a country where getting an education for many girls is made virtually impossible. A male-run extremist group called the Taliban tried to kill her when she and a small group of other girls insisted on going to school. Luckily, she survived being shot in the head and now lives in England, where she is free to learn. Her determination to want to get a good education, even though she knew she may be attacked or even killed for doing so, is unbelievably brave. She jointly won the Nobel Peace Prize, has written a book, and has spoken at the United Nations, a human rights organisation, in New York, on the importance of girls being educated. This girl is an inspiration. She sums up triumph through adversity. She has sparkle. She makes you listen to her, and somehow you just know she will go far.

Thankfully, you do not have to go through the terrible things she did to go far. Just imagine if you did have to, though. Would you be as brave?

two

Fab-U-Cation

I never cut class. I loved getting A's;
I liked being smart. I liked being
on time. I thought being smart was
cooler than anything in the world.
—Michelle Obama, first lady
of the United States

Fab-u-cation? OK, I completely made this word up. But it reminds us what education can do for us. As Michelle Obama says, being smart is cooler than anything in the world.

It's not always easy to get motivated to do schoolwork. Sometimes it seems boring or irrelevant to your life. Classmates can be disruptive and can distract you. Friends may encourage you to bunk off, leaving you behind with lessons.

But there's also much more to contend with at secondary school than just that. These statistics show just what girls going to school every day in the United Kingdom have to cope with on top of the stresses of learning:

- **Seventy-one per cent of sixteen- to eighteen-year-olds say they have heard sexual name-calling, such as "slut" or "slag" towards girls at school daily or a few times per week.**

- **Close to one in three (29 per cent) of sixteen- to eighteen-year-old girls say they have experienced unwanted sexual touching at school.**

- **Close to one in three (28 per cent) of sixteen- to eighteen-year-olds say they have seen sexual pictures on mobile phones at school a few times a month or more.**

- **Close to one in four (24 per cent) of sixteen- to eighteen-year-olds said that their teachers *never* said unwanted sexual touching, sharing of sexual pictures or sexual name-calling are unacceptable.**

- **Forty per cent of sixteen- to eighteen-year-olds said they didn't receive lessons or information on sexual consent or didn't know whether they did.**

(*Source: "2010 poll on sexual harassment in schools," http://www.endviolenceagainstwomen. org.uk/2010-poll-on-sexual-harassment-in-schools*)

How do you deal with all these things and study?

Part of the great challenge of living is defining yourself in your moment, of seizing the opportunities that you are given, and of making the very best choices you can.
—Hillary Clinton

Being able to avoid or handle these problems is the key to success. When you can do that, the rest of life will not seem as scary at all. We will look at all these issues later in the book. Right now, I want to concentrate on what education can do for you.

Not getting a good job when you leave school is bad for you. That's official. The Centre for Social Justice, an organisation that looks at poverty and ways to tackle it in the United Kingdom, says: "Too many young people leave school without the skills and qualifications to secure a sustainable job and lead a fulfilling life."

So why is this the situation when education in this country is free? Are some of you actively discouraged by family who think it's a waste of time? Or is it because *you* think it's pointless and don't bother to study? Maybe you look around where you live and there are no jobs, no money, and, it seems, no way out. *Hello, girls!* Education is your passport out.

> *I was raised to believe that excellence is the best deterrent to racism or sexism. And that's how I operate my life.*
> *—Oprah Winfrey, US actress, TV presenter, and businesswoman*

Be the best you can at what you do, and you will have many more opportunities in life.

Learning helps us to be aware of what is around us and enables us to choose what sort of career we want.

There are thousands of different jobs out there. Thousands. Not just one or two careers such as teacher, nurse, accountant, doctor, shop worker, or call centre worker. There are jobs you never even realised existed connected to every subject you study at school. Just Google "What jobs could I do with a history degree or a geography degree?" and you will see what I mean.

Ever thought about becoming an astronaut, a chocolatier, translator, politician, a make-up artist for TV or films, a hotel manager, a fashion clothes buyer for an exclusive store like Selfridges (or even a big store like Bloomingdale's in New York)? Sound too good to be true? Well, it's not. These are jobs that you could be doing if you put your mind to it. There are many more jobs like them too.

My belief is: if a job exists in this world, there is no reason why you can't do it.

> *My brother, David, was eighteen months older so anything he could do, I wanted to do—and there was never any differentiation between us. My parents never said: "David can go racing and you can stay at home and play with Barbie."*
> *—Susie Wolff, Formula One racing driver*

Do not put up barriers to what is achievable in your life. Someone always has to be the first to achieve something. It could be you. When scientists said they would put a man on the moon, people laughed and said it was impossible. But someone believed they could, and they did.

Until you get inspired to do a particular job or have a certain career, learning at school can seem underwhelming. But education and aspiration is the key to a bright future.

When you know definitely what you want to do, you should feel on fire for it and be excited by the prospect of achieving it. School is just a stepping stone to bigger things.

I haven't met anyone who messed about at school and left with no qualifications who wouldn't love the chance to go back and learn. When you're at school, it's difficult to imagine being all grown up. It will come, and you need to have a plan.

Education brings independence and freedom. It is a freedom we should appreciate. As we know, so many girls do not have your chances.

It was the girl band *Destiny's Child* who hit the nail on the head with their song "Independent Women." These lyrics say it all.

Question: Tell me what you think about me
I buy my own diamonds and I buy my own rings
Only ring your cell-y when I'm feelin' lonely
When it's all over please get up and leave
Question: Tell me how you feel about this
Try to control me boy you get dismissed
Pay my own fun, oh and I pay my own bills
Always fifty-fifty in relationships

The shoes on my feet
I've bought it
The clothes I'm wearing
I've bought it
The rock I'm rockin'
'Cause I depend on me

If I wanted the watch you're wearin'
I'll buy it
The house I live in
I've bought it
The car I'm driving
I've bought it
I depend on me.

Girls, if you want a comfortable lifestyle, you have to go out and earn it. It's just like the song says. You can't expect anyone else to do it for you. Unless you inherit wealth or win the lottery, this is just a fact.

The world is not like a fairy tale. You do not get a fairy godmother; you have to be your own. If you want something, you have to get it for yourself. Education helps you achieve that.

As the song says, empowerment (or "girl power") is about being able to stand on your own two feet. It's about being independent and being able to buy the things you need and want for yourself and your family. What a sense of achievement that sort of independence is! It gives you security and freedom. The best thing about growing up and being an adult is being able to do what you want to do. The only way to truly achieve this is by being financially independent. To be financially independent, you need a good job. You only get a good job or career through education.

Education is the key to unlocking the world, a passport to freedom.
—Oprah Winfrey

Girls, we are bombarded by sexist messages in advertising, storybooks, and films that we need a man to solve all our problems. Think of the children's stories "Cinderella" and "Sleeping Beauty." Without us realising it, we are programmed from an early age to think that a man is the only person who can solve our problems. These stories instil in girls the myth that we are weak on our own. That if only we can find a rich man to marry, we will be fine. They also imply that all men are fantastic, faultless humans whose only desire is to make us happy all the time. No human being is that perfect. Not a man or a woman.

There are no two ways about it; falling in love is great. But when you meet the person you want to spend the rest of your life with, you will have to compromise, you have to discuss things. You will have to talk about your future, where you are going to live, if you are going to have children—and if you do, who will stay at home and look after them.

That time when you leave school, college, or university and start work should be your time to grow into the person you want to be, to be a little selfish if you want and not have to ask for permission or money from anyone to do the things you want to do.

I want you to feel you have lived life and had lots of good experiences before serious commitments land on your plate.

A partner that's worthy of being in your life will be pleased that you are a strong, independent person with a job and career of your own. If they are jealous, controlling, and don't like the fact you work and have ambition, they are not for you. Move on. Don't let anyone into your heart or life who does not make you happy and who does not want the same things for you that you want for yourself.

What we should all want is an equal relationship where our brains are valued just as much as our boobs!

Girls, getting a great education, even here in the United Kingdom, can be far from easy. Going to a good school that is supportive and can help and guide you to success is not a given. You may be lucky and go to a great school, be slightly less lucky and go to an average one, or be very unlucky and go to a terrible one, and there's nothing you can do about that. But you can still achieve your dreams if you're determined and if you push yourself, praise yourself, and keep your eyes firmly fixed on your end goal. If you are struggling or falling behind with lessons, don't be afraid to ask for help from your teachers. They can help you on the road to success, but you may need to go and ask for their help.

> *The big secret in life is that there is no*
> *big secret. Whatever your goal, you can*
> *get there if you're willing to work.*
> *—Oprah Winfrey*

three

Think Big

If you think you're too small to have an impact, try going to bed with a mosquito.
—Anita Roddick, founder of The Body Shop

I hope you do, but not every girl comes from a family that loves and cherishes her. This is a family that thinks she should have the same rights and chances as boys, that she should have a career and be independent, and that she is clever and can grow up to be and do anything she wants.

Even in schools here in the United Kingdom, girls can be written off because of their backgrounds. For example, if you come from a family where brothers and sisters have been through the school and never passed an exam in their lives or who did not seem to want to learn, then the teachers who taught them may think you will be the same. They may assume you will not want to learn or that you are not capable of learning. This can mean you are put on the scrapheap before you have even started!

It may be that you are considered to be from a culture that expects a girl to marry on leaving school and to dedicate herself to her family. If this is the case, then some teachers may think there's no point in encouraging you.

Never let other people's prejudices or their narrow-mindedness put you off. Teachers do the job because they want to help, but sometimes, as I've said, you may need to go and ask for it.

Who your family members are and what they have or have not achieved in their lives should not cast a shadow over you. You are unique. Just because your mum and dad are both accountants doesn't mean you will be one. Or, just because your mum and dad don't work or have never worked doesn't mean you have to be like that either.

In America, they still believe, despite the recent recession, that anyone can rise from a poor background and become the president. They call it "the American dream." But to date, it is the United Kingdom, not the United States, that has had a woman leading the country.

Margaret Thatcher became our first female prime minister in 1979. She came from fairly humble beginnings. Her dad ran a corner shop. She went to one of the best universities in the country and studied chemistry. She then managed to break into the male-dominated world of politics. She did this through sheer hard work and determination. Whether you love or loathe Margaret Thatcher's politics, or don't know much about them, is irrelevant here. I just want you to know that a woman has run our country. She was the first to do it. She will not be the last. Maybe the next woman prime minister could be you?

Of course, it's hugely disappointing all these years later, there has not been another woman prime minister. Politics is still a male-dominated world. Yes, we have more female politicians, but are there many of them in senior roles? No. Men currently outnumber women four to one in Parliament. This is proof that as a woman, the journey to the top to achieve your career dreams will be tougher in many cases than a man's, but it is *not* impossible if you want it enough.

> *I will never give up. I never have, even when times have been terrible.*
> *—Michelle Mone, OBE, one of the United Kingdom's most successful businesswomen*

Maybe you fancy yourself as a brilliant businesswoman? That is great. There are many inspiring examples. Google the likes of Kelly Hoppen, Deborah Meaden, Michelle Mone, Oprah Winfrey,

J. K. Rowling, Hilary Devey, Indra Nooyi, Naomi Campbell, Ursula Burns, and Martha Lane Fox. You have probably never heard of some of them, but they have all made it in a so-called "man's" world. They are super successful. Why? Because they did not give up, and they all think big.

These women all have very different businesses, professions, and backgrounds. Some came from poverty to achieve great things. Some suffered major setbacks along the way. Some are British. Some come from other countries. What they all have in common is enormous amounts of "sparkle." That's confidence, determination, self-belief, aspiration and enormous strength. Not physical strength but emotional strength, and that is what you need for life and in any chosen career. Even if you don't want to be a top businesswoman, go online and have a look at these women's stories, because they will inspire you.

> *It's mythical—there's no glass ceiling. A manicured fist will smash it as easily as a male fist.*
> *—Hilary Devey, multimillionaire businesswoman, founder, chief executive, and chairman of the Pall-Ex Group*

The number of women in the business world stands at a rather pathetic 10.2 per cent. Don't get me started on the amount of women that get to the boardroom, where the big decisions are made. That's very low. While we can blame male chauvinism (male prejudice against women; the belief that men are superior in terms of ability and intelligence) for some of this, some of it is our fault for not aspiring or daring to go there.

However, when women do go there, an amazing thing happens. Not only are we good at it, but we are better than men! It's true. Companies with more women at the top making big decisions were found to outperform their rivals. This proves that women are just as good and in some cases *better* than men at these jobs.

I have never once thought "I can't." When I decided I wanted to become a journalist, it never occurred to me that I wouldn't do it, or that as a woman I would be discriminated against. I just got on with it and kept moving forward until I achieved it. It wasn't easy. At first I got lots of rejection letters. But I didn't give up, and you mustn't either.

Girls, you have to stand up and take what you want from life. Study hard. Go for those jobs that look out of reach. Apply for the promotions that are usually given to men. Yes, women are still being sidelined for the top jobs and are often not paid the same as men, but unless you push your way forward, nothing will ever change. Chauvinism, sexism, call it what you like, is rife in our society. You'll know this from school by the way many boys treat girls. However, this does not mean you should accept it.

Women are like tea bags, you don't know how strong they are until they get in hot water!
—Eleanor Roosevelt

Let's look at school. Girls now do much better in GCSEs and A-Levels, and there are now more women graduating from university than men. Brilliantly, around 60 per cent of new university graduates are women. However, girls are a minority in fields like maths and computing (21 per cent) and in engineering (12 per cent). These areas are where the big earning potential is. Girls are put off because they often feel the courses are "too male." By not choosing these subjects, girls are removing themselves from some of the highest-earning jobs.

Until a few years ago, nurses, pretty much, were always women and doctors men. Thankfully, this has changed. Now more women than men are training to become doctors. There was a time when all police officers were men. When women did join the force, they only made tea and had minor roles. Now they hold very senior jobs. There are women running police forces. Change has happened in many areas, but there is still a long way to go. Don't be put off if sometimes you have to be the pioneer in your chosen career. It's your actions that will encourage more women to follow in your footsteps.

Be aware that there are people who will genuinely want to protect you from failure and will try to talk you out of "thinking big." They will suggest you should be "realistic" and do something easier, something you cannot fail at. They are in some ways thinking of you. They are probably trying to be kind. They don't want you to be hurt should you get knocked back. The fact is, we all suffer knock-backs. It's just a fact of life. Don't take rejection personally. You must get back up again and keep going. No one wants to think that during their lives, "What if I had tried a bit harder? Maybe I would have achieved my ambition." **Failure is not bad. Not trying is!**

On that very subject, careers guidance at school is very mixed and can be a bit narrow-minded. When I said I wanted to be a journalist, I was persuaded to think again, as "It is a very difficult career to get into." Yes, that's true, but I knew that I wanted to do it and I wasn't going to let one person's opinion or the fact it wasn't a particularly easy career to get into put me off. I knew it was for me and that I would be good at it. I was prepared to ignore advice and plough on to achieve my dream, and you should be too.

> *I think you can have it all, you just*
> *have to work really hard because*
> *great things don't come easily.*
> *—Katy Perry, pop star*

Sometimes, well-meaning career advisors can try to pigeonhole you into certain jobs. I know of people who have grown up in an area known for manufacturing, and on that basis it was automatically assumed that the pupils would go to work at the nearby factory after school, so they were encouraged to study the subjects that would get them jobs there. No one bothered to ask what the students' dreams were or helped them pursue them.

Do not let your options be limited by the closed minds of those around you. Do not let others' opinions of you set you up for a life of failure or underachievement. "Be realistic" is a phrase that makes me mad. What does being realistic really mean? When people use it, they seem to mean to dilute people's dreams. If people were realistic, we would never have got to the moon, invented the Internet, or pioneered medical transplants that save thousands of lives a year. It is the "unrealistic" people who get amazing things done.

Girls, we have a tendency to be discouraged by others. If we fail at something the first time, it's easy to just write ourselves off as useless and give up. Keep going. Virtually no one successful had success straight away. They learned from their mistakes and got there in the end. I had lots of rejection letters from newspapers when I wrote asking for a job as a trainee reporter at the start of my career. Yes, it was upsetting. Yes, it hurt my pride, but I got over it. I refused to take no for an answer, and it worked. Perseverance will work for you too.

This quote sums up what I am talking about, and it's so true.

Whether you think you can, or you think you can't—you're right.
—Henry Ford, businessman and founder of the Ford Motor Company

If you put your mind into a "can-do" mode, you will achieve what it is you are trying to do. You probably know from small things, like when you are doing sports and stop too long to think, "Can I really run and jump over that hurdle in one go?" It is the doubt that stops you. However, when you don't think about it and just go for it, you clear it easily.

Your mind has an incredible effect on your achievements. Put positive things in, and you will get positive things out. Put negative things in, and guess what? Negative stuff comes out.

We can talk ourselves in and out of all sorts of things if we think too long about them. We can sabotage ourselves by thinking we cannot do something before we have even tried!

You are young, and at this age, you can work towards being anything you want, achieving anything you want to. All you have to do is decide what you want from life and then slowly and steadily work towards getting it. Your life is just starting, and that's exciting.

> *No pessimist ever discovered the secret of the stars or sailed an uncharted land, or opened a new doorway for the human spirit.*
> *—Helen Keller (1880–1968), US political activist, author and humanitarian*

Helen Keller was the first deaf and blind person to get a bachelor of arts degree. This woman was amazing. Google her!

I'm pretty sure when the athlete and Olympic gold medal winner Jessica Ennis-Hill was training hard, she never thought that training morning and night for hours was pointless. She knew that to achieve, she had to do the groundwork. She was totally focused. She wanted to win an Olympic gold medal and be the best in the world at her sport. It was her determination, self-belief, and passion that led her to that success.

The feeling of being up on that Olympic podium and being handed a gold medal in front of the whole world must have been pure ecstasy. Her hard work has not just brought her sporting glory but fame and fortune. She knows more than anyone that discipline and hard work does pay off, even when things don't go right all the time, and it can for you too.

I'm proud of the way I've dealt with set-backs. It's hard when you feel down and you think, "Why is the world doing this to me?" But you have to pick yourself up again. That's what makes you a better athlete.
—Jessica Ennis-Hill, athlete, Olympic champion

It's brilliant if you can decide on a career or know what you want to do when you are young. It can give you the purpose you need to get through the mountains of schoolwork you are faced with, or the sports training if your goal is to be a sportswoman, or music practise if your goal is to be a musician.

If you don't know what you would like to do when you leave school, you need to start thinking. Don't settle for your second-best choice either, just because you don't think you'll be able to achieve your first choice. Go for the thing you really want. You may change your mind about what that thing is along the way, but always go for the thing you *really* want rather than the thing that would be easier to achieve. You will be grateful in the end. Even if it takes longer or it's harder.

No matter how terrible a day you are having, or how badly you have done in tests or exams, keep on trying. Where you are now may seem a million miles away from where you want to be, but that's

OK. Keep working towards it and focus on the end result you want.

> *What we find is that if you have a goal that is very, very far out, and you approach it in little steps, you start to get there faster. Your mind opens up to the possibilities.*
> *—Mae Jemison, first African American female astronaut*

Do not let people hold you back because they cannot understand your dream for your life.

four

Being Fabulous

Figure out who you are separate from your family and the man or woman you're in a relationship with. Find who you are in this world and what you need to feel good alone. I think that's the most important thing in life. Find a sense of self because with that, you can do anything else.
—Angelina Jolie, Oscar-winning actress, film director and producer, and human rights campaigner

I didn't write this chapter, "Being Fabulous," about looking like a supermodel. I mean being a strong, confident, happy girl who grows into a confident woman, a girl who expects from the world the same as any boy. A girl who believes in herself and who doesn't need any boy or society to tell her she looks good to make her feel good, because she knows it herself already.

To me, a "sense of self" means seeing the world and understanding that it doesn't always work in your favour but not letting it define you or put you off. It's also recognising the difference between being empowered and a victim.

Being fabulous means learning how to cope with growing up and how to protect yourself both physically and emotionally. It's about being resilient. That's the ability to recover quickly from any difficulties. That's a massive asset to have in this world.

Being fabulous is also thinking for yourself and making decisions that are right for *you*, not to please others.

It's easy to be influenced about how to look, how to have relationships, and how to define what love and sex are. There are so many views on all these things in magazines, on social media, and from friends. Many are misleading, and some are downright wrong and even harmful.

At a time when you are trying to find your way as a young woman and fit into a grown-up world, you are being bombarded by all sorts of mixed messages.

We are led to believe that, thanks to feminist campaigners of the past, life is much better for girls and women nowadays and much more fair and equal. In some ways, it is. But are we being conned into thinking we have achieved all there is to achieve? Is the reality that these achievements are now subtly being taken away from us?

It seems to me that there are two types of equality right now: true equality and fake equality.

True equality promotes girls in a positive light and gives girls freedom to be and do what they want and to be equal to boys. This type of equality has no negative side. Fake equality is where we are conned into acting or behaving a certain way because we believe we are empowered and liberated by doing so when the reality is the opposite.

What equality is considered to be, it seems to me, is going backwards in some cases. Attitudes towards girls are getting worse. Just look at the statistic I quoted in the introduction to this book: **one in two boys thinks it is OK to hit a girl sometimes or to force her to have sex!**

It is a sad fact that reported rapes of women in England and Wales are up by 31 per cent. There were more than 24,000 incidents reported in the 12 months to September 2014. **(Source: Office for National Statistics)**. Many are not reported. According to rapecrisis.org.uk around 85,000 women and girls are raped each year. On the one hand, girls are encouraged to be sexier and more daring than ever, but on the other hand, it seems that when we are, we are punished for it.

Women asked for equality. We did not ask to be abused.

Women won control over whether to have a baby or not in the 1960s when the contraceptive pill was invented. Other forms of contraception were used before this but not many of them were as reliable or easily available to women. Women had to rely on men for contraception. Being able to use the contraceptive pill meant that women had control. They could enjoy sex without fear of getting pregnant when they didn't want to. Before this, single women getting pregnant outside marriage were shunned and looked down on by many in society. (This of course, still happens). The pill also allowed married women to control how many babies they had. This was good for their health, as having lots of children can be damaging to some women's health. It was also good for families' economic situations, as having lots of children to feed and clothe left many families in terrible poverty. So this reliable form of contraception allowed women to have more equality with men and improved their lives. It was also their choice whether to take it or not. Some women choose not to take it for religious reasons and as with all medication, there can be side effects.

Interestingly, two big firms in America recently announced they are willing to pay for some female employees to freeze the eggs from their wombs so they can delay motherhood. For pregnancy, a man's sperm fertilises a woman's egg inside her womb. The quality of a woman's eggs deteriorates as she gets older, making it harder and harder for older women to become pregnant. So, in theory, egg freezing means that the eggs don't deteriorate, and if reimplanted in the woman, it should mean she is more easily able to have a healthy baby when she is older. It also means, in theory, that women can keep working and hold on to their dreams of being mothers until much later in life.

But is this empowering for women or actually a subtle way to control them? Rather than women deciding for themselves when they are ready for a baby, does this mean companies are deciding for them?

Egg freezing is an expensive procedure, and so it may look like the firm is being generous. But remember, they are offering this so-called "perk" not just to be nice but because they, presumably, would prefer not to lose valuable female employees. Offering women the chance to freeze their eggs means they will not have to stop work for maternity leave. They will be inclined to work longer and to park motherhood. That is great for the company. It can be a great idea for the woman too if she has no partner or is not ready to have children.

What concerns me is that women may feel pressured into egg freezing or think it's what is expected of them if they want to keep their high-flying jobs. This offer, as good as it may look, can also bring a slight threat too. This may not be the intention of the company at all, but it could be how a woman may see it.

As I say, there might not be any actual pressure by the company to freeze eggs, but the subtle message it sends out to the female workforce may make them feel they must delay motherhood if they want to succeed.

If more companies offer women employees egg freezing, is society in danger of telling women when they should be having babies instead of them choosing for themselves? Does it turn a natural process into a costly and uncomfortable medicalised one?

Having a baby is an emotional yearning, not just a process, and we have to consider the emotional harm this could potentially have on some women.

The whole idea of equality is fairness for women. As I have said, egg freezing can be useful for some women, but there are concerns too. For example, if a woman does feel pressured to delay motherhood, imagine how upsetting it could be to see male colleagues the same age as her becoming fathers. This makes women less equal to men in the workplace. It might also create tensions.

The process of having your eggs removed from your womb and frozen is an invasive medical procedure. It's time-consuming and can be painful. It's not easy and quick, and like any type of surgery, it does carry risks. So, should you choose to put yourself through this medical ordeal, make sure it really is to please and benefit you and not your employer.

There is also the possibility that women may be being misled into thinking that freezing their eggs will guarantee them a baby should they decide they want one. This is not a definite. It's trickier to produce a baby using frozen eggs than naturally. Therefore, the female employee may find herself in the potentially devastating situation that she has missed out on being a mother altogether. Who do you blame then? Yourself for going along with idea, or your firm for giving you the option? There is no clear answer to this, but I am sure you can see it's not a good position to be in, so it may be best not to get into that situation in the first place. At least, think very seriously about it first.

Egg freezing *is* valuable for women who are facing medical treatment for illnesses such as cancer, where the drugs to treat the illness affect a woman's fertility and ability to have a baby. There are downsides and good sides to everything. You have to work out what works for you.

This whole scenario is just one example of what I mean when I ask, "Is feminism in reverse?" On one hand, a firm paying for egg freezing looks like a great help, but on the other, it can be seen as a form of control. It's so subtle that we may not even realise it. Only if you understand this and consider all sides can you make an informed choice.

Looking good and feeling fabulous

Celebrity culture and our image-obsessed media are constantly telling girls how they should look to be considered attractive. We are shown pictures of female celebrities who have lost weight, and they are praised for being thin. We see pictures of female celebrities who have put weight on, and they are criticised for getting fat. Neither of these is an ultimate goal. Being fit and healthy and happy is what we should strive for.

Women and girls are routinely judged on every aspect of how they look. Boys are too but it is girls that are put under the microscope. Society puts out the message that you must look a certain way to be considered worthwhile as a human being. **It subtly sends the message that girls don't need to worry about having a brain if they look a certain way.** This means that many girls might decide not to study or will see learning as irrelevant. This is disastrous. A lack of qualifications can make it very hard to get a good job. So the very idea that society promotes that women should concentrate on looking good can end up trapping women in poverty.

Women who do work hard and have ambition can also be harmed by this thinking. They might not be taken seriously in their workplace because men think that brains and beauty are impossible to find in the same woman. This sexist attitude can stop us from being fabulous if we fall for it.

Girls, life is not about looking like a Barbie doll. A doll has no feelings and no brains. Life is about being your fabulous self and being appreciated and liked for the kind of person you are rather than for your looks. It's worth mentioning here that there's also considerable pressure on women not to look old. Looks may change as we get older, but it doesn't mean that you can't be fabulous at any age. You can.

Society considers older men with grey hair distinguished, experienced, and even sometimes sexy. Many hold down powerful jobs. Grey-haired older women are virtually invisible in our society.

The grey-haired professor Mary Beard, who presents a history programme on TV, was inundated with a torrent of vile abuse by trolls on social media when she appeared on a political discussion programme. Why are we so full of hate and ready to dismiss an older woman when she's on TV when grey-haired older men are on TV all the time, and quite rightly, their looks are never mentioned? This is sexist.

In fact, in the sea of seminaked images we see around us in the media, most are women, and pretty perfect ones. Adverts, glossy magazines, and pop videos are full of glamorous women who are made to look totally perfect thanks to whizz-bang technology (usually Photoshop, or the like) that erases wrinkles and spots, makes waists smaller and legs longer or slimmer. These pictures create fake women who don't exist in the real world. They can make us feel inferior.

A woman's character is killed off by this blurring and mending of features. As well as the whole body-confidence issue this creates, it also sends out the dangerous messages that A, the woman is not attractive enough to go on the cover of a magazine as she is and B, it doesn't matter how talented you are if you're female. Brains and talent come second to your looks.

Of course, boys and men worry about their looks too, but there's not nearly so much pressure and sexualisation of their bodies. They certainly are not treated the same way girls and women are.

It's no wonder, then, that the 2014 British Social Attitudes survey by NatCen Social Research reveals that **only 63 per cent of women aged 18 to**

34 and 57 per cent of women aged 35 to 49 are satisfied with their appearance.

It also found that **three-quarters of adults think that society puts too much pressure on females to have a sexualised appearance** and that **nearly half of all adults think that "how you look affects what you can achieve in life."** One-third agree with the statement, **"Your value as a person depends on how you look."**

These beliefs can have a very damaging effect on how we feel about ourselves. If all our emotions are focused on obsessing about how we look, we can end up descending into self-loathing. It can also lead many straight to the nearest cosmetic surgeon!

The number of young women choosing to undergo painful operations to change their appearance has risen dramatically. Many women say they want surgery to help boost their self-esteem because they don't like the way they look. Yet no one asks what has caused this self-hatred in the first place.

Cosmetic surgery costs a lot. Thousands of pounds. Many women are not only undergoing unnecessary procedures that carry potential risks, they are also putting themselves in debt to pay for them.

This, to me, is a double insult. Not only is it painful to be told by our looks-obsessed culture that we must look a certain way, but women also face the financial pain of going into debt to pay for the operations!

The cosmetic surgery business is expected to be worth £3.6 billion in 2015.

Of course, cosmetic surgery can do amazing things. In cases where women have had breasts removed because of cancer or where someone has a deformity that can be improved, it can be brilliant. Then it really can boost self-esteem, and that can change a life. What should concern us is that young women are having alterations to their faces and bodies when there is absolutely no need. After all, all surgery carries risks. It can go wrong. Why would you want to put yourself through that?

Look what happened when it was found that many women had been given breast implants that were filled with low-grade mattress stuffing. It caused fear and distress for thousands of women all worried about their health. In a separate incident, one British woman recently died having liposuction surgery abroad.

Cosmetic surgery is being seen as the norm nowadays, a bit like buying a new outfit!

The British Association of Aesthetic Plastic Surgeons says they are seeing more young people who want cosmetic surgery. They've warned that young patients can be vulnerable and often have self-esteem issues. They say surgery is often too big a thing for them to go through.

There's no doubt that pressure on young women to look a certain way, a fake way, is driving them to have operations and procedures they do not need, cannot afford, and could go wrong. Let's not forget that they're painful too. There is also the very real possibility you will not look exactly as you had hoped. I would question why young women would want to put themselves through this without medical need.

By the way, it may come as no surprise that very few men have cosmetic surgery.

Loathing our bodies is so damaging and a waste of our precious time. When I've been out clothes shopping, I've heard young girls moan about their bodies and call themselves fat when they're not at all. These are dangerous, negative feelings. They stop you being the fabulous girl you are right now and enjoying your life.

Other people will always have something to say about how we look. We have to be able to ignore it and get on with being us. When you wear something, wear it for you and because you feel great in it.

If the way you look concerns you or you want advice on how to cope if you are being bullied about your appearance, go to changingfaces.org.uk. It's a charity that has self-help guides for children and young people on these issues.

Politicians from all parties are so concerned about the pressure on people to look a certain way that they commissioned a report on body image. It found that **girls as young as five are worrying about their size and appearance** and that **one in four seven-year-old girls have tried to lose weight at least once.**

To feel fabulous, we need to be kind to ourselves, like ourselves, and find ourselves attractive as we are. I know it sounds bizarre, but it's true.

We need to like what we see in the mirror. Don't dwell on what you would rather see there. Remember, as a teenager, your body is going to be changing for a while yet, so don't stress about looking grown-up. You are still growing. Your features will change for some years to come.

Let's tackle this mirror issue. When you look in the mirror, what do you see? What do you like about your looks? If you can't say anything nice, then you are not alone, but you are in trouble. Girls, we are too hard on ourselves, and we need to stop it right away. You can't feel confident and ready to make your mark on the world or get your plans together if you don't feel good about yourself. Feeling fabulous is important.

All women and girls go through stages when they dislike things about themselves. Often, though, our obsessive hates about ourselves are not even noticed by our friends. That's because we often blow them out of proportion—or they don't exist!

When I think about why girls are putting so much pressure on themselves, it's usually because they want to be accepted by society, look attractive, and be liked by boys. This is negative. *You* have to like you.

> *I come across too much material on "how to make a man want you," "how to make a man commit," "how to make a man finally pop the question," "how to make a man take you seriously," "how to get into a man's emotions." And I laugh. My dear fellow women, enough! Do not busy yourselves with such things! Instead, fall in love with yourself!*
> *—C. JoyBell C., author*

What I would like you to do now is look at yourself in a mirror and say what you like about your looks. You might be thinking, "That's easy—nothing!" Now, that's not true. Look again. Come up with at least three things. You shouldn't be struggling here. It could be that you like your eyes or your hair or your smile.

Now stand away from the mirror and think about what you like about your personality. Are you fun to be around? Are you kind? Are you thoughtful? These are all things that make you you. They also make you attractive and likeable to those around you.

How you are as a person, not how you *look*, is what makes you truly fabulous.

I am sure this exercise will take some of you ages to do, but if I asked you to tell me what is attractive about your best friend, you would probably do it straight away. Your best friend would probably be able to come up with a whole list of things that are attractive about you too. Try it. It will make you both feel good.

When you are at school, image is very important. Puberty can be cruel. We get hairy, start periods, and get spots. Just remember that everyone is going through it too. Some may sail through this time more easily than others, but they're not going to escape it.

We live in a sexist and highly pressurised world that tells us all the time to look a certain way if we want to be liked. But it tells girls this much more than boys. Take the music industry. It is the female artists who are most often seen wearing virtually nothing. Not many male pop stars strip down to their underwear to sell a record.

> *I make music to be a musician, not*
> *to be on the cover of a Playboy.*
> *—Adele Adkins, musician and*
> *multi award-winning singer*

Interestingly, Adele Adkins, who never takes her clothes off on stage, has turned out to be one of our biggest and most talented musicians and singers. Beyoncé too is a strong female role model. Both are beautiful. They do not look like a thousand other women. They are not stick thin. They prove that you do not have to look a certain way to be attractive and successful.

There are many types of beautiful. If we all looked the same, it would be a dull and boring world. Please remember this when you stare at the mirror, complaining about what you see!

This report shows how girls struggle with body image:

While alone in a dressing room, college students were asked to try on either a swimsuit or a sweater. While they waited for ten minutes wearing the garment, they completed a maths test. The results revealed that the young women in swimsuits performed significantly worse on the maths problems than those wearing sweaters. No differences were found for young men.

*(**Source: Report of the American Psychological Association on the Sexualisation of Girls, 2010**)*

In other words, thinking about their body and worrying about how they looked disrupted the girls' brainpower. This report shows that how we look and *feel* we look can have a damaging effect on our education and well-being.

One study in the report looked at the "throwing like a girl" stereotype. It found that, compared with boys, girls tend not to bring their whole bodies into a throw. This isn't because we can't. It's just that girls aged ten through to seventeen were so concerned about how their bodies looked that they didn't put their all into the throw. **This shows that a lack of confidence and fear of how others are judging our bodies can hold us back from doing the things we want to do. Don't let it.**

The funny thing is that if you put your all into a throw, you will probably throw well. When you throw well, people will not be looking at your body, but they will be thinking of how well you play. Please do not let your inhibitions make you give up sport. Sport is for everyone, no matter what shape and size.

If I hear another girl say she has given up sport because she gets sweaty and does not look good, I think I will go mad. Who says you have to look great all the time? When I am doing sport, for example, I wear no make-up and go bright red. I resemble a tomato. It is not attractive to me or anyone else, but I do not care. It makes me feel good.

> *It's so important girls don't drop fitness in their teens. Fitness protects us from ill health, heads off issues around weight, appearance and obesity and it helps to curb excesses. A good sport experience is confidence giving…*
> *—Liz Nicoll, OBE, chief executive officer, UK Sport*

Antisocial Media?

To feel fabulous and be your fabulous true self, you have to feel confident. This leads me to the subject of social media. Yes, we all love it. I know you're probably addicted to BBM messaging on your mobile phone, Facebook, Twitter, Instagram, and the many other sites.

I am not saying don't use it. I'd be a hypocrite if I said that. Social media is part of our modern culture. I use it. I enjoy it. You can do so much on the Internet. You can have a blog. Make friends with others who share your interests. Set up a business (many young people have). Learn all sorts of fantastic stuff and connect with other young people in a way girls your age never could before.

I keep quoting websites and suggesting you look up people I've quoted, so I know the Internet is a fantastic research tool. But we all know it has a dark side too.

Social media is a strange, new world. Experts are only just starting to do studies on whether it is good or bad for us or what effect it's having on our brains and whether it leads to an inability to concentrate. For a start, most people on social media talk rubbish. Personally, I don't care if someone has had a row with a boyfriend and changed his or her status to single. I don't care what someone has had for breakfast. I can understand why some experts are concerned that this sort of exposure and constant immersion in such inane drivel will make us stupid.

It's also a world where we often divulge our innermost thoughts, but do we really know who we're sharing that information with?

The average twelve- to-fifteen-year-old has never met one in four of their "friends" on social networking sites. (*Source: Ofcom*)

It's a world where you never really know who your friends are.

We live in a society that rewards exhibitionism. Just look at the rise of the selfie. Most of the time, it's harmless. But it's tempting to say too much and share too much on social media. It's easy to fall into the trap of feeling comfortable doing so when you are cocooned in the safety of your bedroom.

Flinders University in Australia carried out some research on this involving more than a thousand school-age girls. They found that teenage conversations about appearance were "intensified" on social media and more influential because they involved peers.

Experts from the university found that time spent on social network sites was related to lower self-esteem, lower body esteem, a weaker sense of identity, and higher depression.

Social media can be fun. It's an important tool used by many businesses, and it can be informative. News organisations, politicians, and charities all use it to get their thoughts out to the wider population. But it can also badly misinform. There are so many sites that are not reputable and that give out misleading information. Sites that encourage girls to obsess about weight and looks are rife and can cause terrible self-loathing. There are sites that incite people to self-harm or even hurt others. We all have to be very careful about what we look at and what we "learn" from social media.

We live in a country that allows free speech, and that is great, but it does mean that anyone can go online and spout their own personal views on any issue. Be aware that even sites that may seem official may misinform.

Social media is very useful when it comes to following organisations and people who make a difference, so have a good look at your list of social media friends. Weed out the ones you don't know personally or who say dodgy things. Use the privacy settings. Switch your phone off sometimes, especially when you go to bed. Take a mind break. Don't be a slave to social media or the Internet. Make them work for *you*.

Don't Be Afraid to Make a Noise

Being fabulous sometimes means having to make a big noise.

A report by the National Society for the Prevention of Cruelty to Children (NSPCC) shows that girls at school are having to put up with more and more sexual harassment from boys. The report says that there is **"a deeply rooted notion that girls and young women's bodies are somehow the property of boys and young men." (*Source: NSPCC*. A Qualitative Study of Children, Young People and "Sexting")**

This is grim. You are not the property of anyone. You live in a free country. You are in charge of your body. No one else is. It can be difficult to remember this when so-called "lad culture" is so celebrated.

Just listen to some of the lyrics in rock, rap, gangsta rap, and hip-hop songs. They are mind blowing in their outright misogyny (hatred of women). The songs routinely describe girls as "bitches" and "hoes." When did that become acceptable? These demeaning lyrics are now becoming part of the normal vocabulary of many boys. The fact that they are being used in everyday conversation normalises this sexist attitude and it chips away at girls' self-esteem.

The main message in many songs is that girls exist to be used by boys, and they can use them as and when they want and then chuck them away like rubbish. These lyrics constantly tell boys that they are in control of girls. These songs are empty of human feeling or affection. The sex they talk about in the songs is sometimes abusive. The woman always submissive to the man. The whole act of sex is talked about as if it is inconsequential, it means nothing. The videos show women in bikinis parading around men who are fully dressed, all seemingly vying for the men's attention. This is sexist.

I don't know how music got so full of hatred, but I do believe it's having a negative effect on the sorts of relationships that are developing between many boys and girls. If boys keep hearing these lyrics from their idols, it's only natural that they will think like that too. If girls keep hearing them, it's only logical that many girls too will come to think the behaviour they talk about is normal and acceptable.

The music may be great, and we are all guilty of enjoying music and not taking much notice of the lyrics sometimes, but as girls, we surely cannot agree with what these songs are saying and the influence they are having on boys' behaviour towards girls.

Boys are not being taught to think about your feelings. They are not even being taught that you have any! Everything around them, from porn on the Internet to sexting on social media and these demeaning songs, educates boys to think that girls are objects to use however they want. How do you change that? You change it like anything bad that ever got changed. You demand to be treated better and you make a big noise about it.

The boys behaving like this are teenagers like you. They have no experience about real sex and real relationships. They too are influenced by social media, music, and sexist behaviour around them. They are struggling to make sense of growing up and what it means to be a man. Underneath their big talk, they are vulnerable to criticism too. Their hormones are raging. Some will be pressured into behaving the way they do to fit in with the rest of their mates. That doesn't make their behaviour OK. Girls, if you want to stamp it out, you have to make it very clear that you're not willing to be treated badly. Only by speaking up can you change this negative attitude that some boys have about girls.

All around the world, from Egypt to India and Pakistan and parts of Africa, we are hearing in news reports and from charities about how women are being sexually assaulted as they walk down the road and sometimes even raped in the streets. These are horrifying acts. Of course, not all men in these countries carry out these crimes. In fact, many men are campaigning with women to stop this happening. However, the fact that it is happening, and so blatantly, shows a growing and worrying disregard for women right across the world.

The NSPCC report I've referred to on sexting shows that many girls do not want to perform sex acts or sext pictures of their naked body parts to boys but feel that they have no choice but to do so. They feel that they will be excluded from the "in crowd" or bullied and abused if they don't do it. This is making matters even worse. Not only is this turning girls into playthings for boys, it is leaving them feeling humiliated and inferior.

It's easy to see a connection between degrading rap songs and the real-life treatment of girls. It's turning girls into second-class citizens. When boys get away with behaviour like this, they come to believe that they have power over girls not just physically and sexually, but also in the workplace and generally.

Just being at school can leave you open to this kind of abuse. Sex assaults on girls by boys at school used to be extremely rare. That kind of threat was something that came from strangers. Now, though, the situation is very different.

There are a growing number of sexual assaults by boys on girls at school. Girls in the NSPCC report said they had been physically assaulted. They described being tripped up and pushed down and then being groped or "daggered." This is when a boy rubs themselves up against a girl as if having sex. It is also known as "dry humping".

One girl, aged thirteen, told researchers that she could not expect to walk past boys in the corridor without them touching her, either squeezing her bum or touching her boobs.

These incidents are never acceptable, and they are having a numbing and negative effect on girls. How can you feel fabulous and have sparkle with all this going on? You do not and should not have to put up with it.

The NSPCC report also shows that many girls are now not wearing skirts to school because of

groping by boys. Some girls reported that if they wear a skirt, they also wear shorts underneath for extra protection, to make them "less vulnerable". Girls, it seems, are adapting to this behaviour towards them by changing themselves rather than stopping the problem. This is horrific. No girl should have to go to these lengths to stop being abused. If this is happening to you and your friends at school and you cannot stop it, you have to report it at home to your parents as well as at school. Don't let it be laughed off as boys being boys. I suggest you write down every time it happens, detailing where it happened and who did it. Give one copy of this to your teacher and one to your parents. You are not being a grass. You are being strong and standing up for your rights.

If you as girls cannot go to school or work or just walk down the street without being treated like sex objects, we are living in not only a very unequal society but a backward one too. Girls, it's important that you make a noise about this abusive behaviour. Otherwise, it will not stop. Nothing changes unless you demand change. Tell your teachers. If they don't know about it, they can't stop it.

Talk to other girls and maybe even get a group together to meet and debate this issue. Decide what you want to do about it. Tell your teachers what you are doing and ask if you can hold an assembly to discuss the problem with the whole school.

You could set up a "zero tolerance on harassment and groping at school" campaign. Put up posters telling boys to keep their hands to themselves. Shame them, but more importantly, educate them into behaving better. Get some boys to join your campaign. If none of that works, then hold a protest before or after school outside the school gates. Invite the local media. This will get you publicity for your campaign and get the issue talked about more widely.

It's only when things are out in the open that change happens. You have a right to be heard. You have a right to be treated equally and fairly. Don't be ashamed to speak out. The shame isn't yours but belongs to the boys doing it and the adults who fail to educate both boys and girls to know that this behaviour is wrong and fail to act to stop it.

Don't think you can't change this behaviour. Girls, if you stick together, you can change anything. This has been the case all through history. Don't stay quiet and hide your misery. School is meant to be a place of safety for all, a place of learning, a place where your self-esteem should be allowed to grow, not be battered into the ground because the sexual behaviour of some boys is getting out of hand. It is society's duty to keep children safe.

I think this amazing poem sums up the inequalities that women everywhere face.

Too many women in too many countries
speak the same language of silence.
My grandmother was always silent, always
aggrieved
Only her husband had the cosmic right (or so
it was said)
to speak and be heard.
They say it is different now.
(After all, I am always vocal and my grandmother
thinks I talk too much)
But sometimes I wonder.
When a woman shares her thoughts, as some
women do,
graciously, it is allowed.
When a woman fights for power, as all women
would like
to, quietly or loudly, it is questioned.
And yet, there must be freedom—if we are to
speak
And yes, there must be power—if we are to be
heard.
And when we have both (freedom and power)
let us now be
understood.
We seek only to give words to those who cannot
speak
(too many women in too many countries)
I seek to forget the sorrows of my grandmother's silence.

—*Anasuya Sengupta, poet, activist, and social
scientist*

Being fabulous is about refusing to put up with any behaviour that leaves you humiliated, frightened, or abused. Do not keep quiet about it. That will only hide it.

Being fabulous is about believing you can change things and having the determination to do it.

It is tough being a girl sometimes, but it's also fabulous.

five
Generation Porn

What's sex like? What does love mean? It's an unknown world, something exciting yet to be discovered. What's it like to have a boyfriend and pucker up for that first, lingering kiss? The butterflies in the tummy and the heart racing when you even just talk to someone you really fancy can be thrilling.

But a lack of proper sex education and relationship advice means your generation has got it tough when it comes to working out what it's really all about. There's so much out there to misinform you about what sex is, and some of the problem is down to the huge amount of online porn. Porn is adult fantasy. It is not meant as a tool to teach you about sex.

Porn puts girls, and boys too, at a big disadvantage. It shows a very macho and one-sided look at sex. It says that if you don't look like the perfect people having sex in the film, then you are inferior and inadequate. This can deeply affect how you feel about yourselves and your bodies. Porn does not teach boys or girls how to have a relationship or what love and respect is. It teaches girls that they are sexual objects, and it teaches boys that too. The sort of sex you see in some of the films can also be extreme. It is not the norm for most people or what many people would want to do.

According to a report by the charity Zero Tolerance, 74 per cent of boys watch porn compared with 12 per cent of girls. Smartphone technology means that some children are even watching this stuff at school! **The legal age to watch porn is eighteen.**

It is healthy and perfectly normal to be curious about sex with all your hormones firing off around your body. What is not healthy or helpful for boys or girls is to learn about it from porn.

Most porn sells the myth that sex is something done *to* a woman *by* a man for *his* pleasure. That is a lie. Sex should be pleasurable for both a man and woman. It *is* emotional, and it should involve mutual respect, love, and kindness.

Boys watching porn from a young age can mean that they want to copy what they see and even have sex much earlier than they would if they didn't watch porn. This can have long-lasting effects, especially on girls.

The NSPCC, the children's charity, reports that girls who have sex at a young age are at risk of suffering from low self-esteem and possibly developing mental health issues.

Sex doesn't need to mess your head up. It's certainly not something you have to rush to do. But you do need to know all the facts.

Before I go any further, I want to point out that the legal age to have sex is sixteen. It's a fact that many of you won't feel ready to have sex, even at sixteen, and that is fine. Everyone is different. What I want you to know more than anything is that having sex should be *your* decision—no one else's.

So let us get a few things clear:

- **You don't have to have sex just because your friends are or because you feel pressured into it.**

- **Sex is not just for boys, and it is not something you have to do to make boys like you.**

- **Sex is meant to be just as pleasurable for a woman as a man, and when you do have sex, you are allowed to enjoy it too.**

- **Sex is not a service that you as girls are there to provide whether you want to or not.**

- **Sex is a mutual desire, and most importantly, it is something you should really want to do just as much as the boy.**

- **Violence or being forced to have sex is rape. It is a serious crime that must be reported.**

- **Sex is emotional. Feelings do come into it.**

Anyone who thinks that porn teaches them all they need to know about sex is bonkers. It is more likely to damage relationships between boys and girls because boys are seeing the women in these porn films treated as objects rather than as their equals. This means that they are likely to treat you the same way. They think this is normal.

The NSPCC reports that young people are being bullied by peers into sexual activities they do not want.

There has been an increase in reports of abusive relationships between teenagers. This is not healthy. **Relationships are not meant to be like this.**

These statistics may not be directly related to the rise in young boys watching porn, but seeing sex portrayed in a way that is controlling and emotionless doesn't help.

Sex with someone you care about and who cares about you should never make you feel bad about yourself. It should be a fun and a wonderful experience and one that should make you feel happy and good about yourself.

Violence and forcing someone to have sex is always wrong. **It is a crime.** A young woman who really wants to have sex does not need persuading. She decides for herself. If you say no, it means *no*. No *never* means yes.

Just look at it this way. If you force someone to do something they don't want to do because they are too frightened to say no, that is not a respectful relationship. It's abuse. It's a form of control. There is no respect or love in that relationship. It is one person controlling another, and that is a bad relationship.

I am definitely not a prude when it comes to sex. None of us would be here without it! But I am concerned that as girls, you should know you have a right to an equal sexual relationship and truly understand what that is. Sex is emotional, and you are allowed to enjoy it.

Chapter 9 has some useful websites that will answer all your questions about sex and provide you with honest and reliable advice.

Boy Meets Girl

A few years ago, life for teenagers was simpler. There was no Internet, no social media, and no such thing as a smartphone, so that meant no Internet porn or "sexting." It made life a lot simpler. It gave boys and girls the chance to get to know and understand each other. Everything they said to each other had to be done face-to-face or by speaking to each other over the home telephone. They had to have proper conversations, not just hide behind texts or social media.

It went a bit like this: boy met girl (or, if you like, girl met boy), and they started "going out." They became official girlfriend and boyfriend. They did this because they liked each other. (What a shock!) They got to know each other, maybe shared the same taste in music, sport, or whatever. They cared about what each other thought about them, and yes (shock, horror!), they were nice to each other and respected each other. They held hands and had sneaky snogs. They went out together on "dates"—maybe to the cinema, bowling, the park, to each other's houses. They fumbled up jumpers and skirts and down trousers and learnt to kiss. And when the novelty wore off, they broke up, usually after a few intense weeks together. During all this, they each felt an emotional connection to the other person.

It was very intimate because you really got to learn about each other. It gave boys and girls the chance to really get to know each other. This kind of relationship builds closeness and trust. There was also no fear of humiliation or bullying over the Internet or having your intimate moments published for everyone to see, not just because the Internet didn't exist but also because those moments were private, between just those two people.

This sort of dating ritual taught young people how to act with each other and importantly that dating means an equal relationship. Today's increasingly sexist behaviour by many boys and in society means that you are often being robbed of finding out what a real relationship really should be like. Boys are too. If your only experiences of relationships and sex are from porn, that's not much of a surprise.

A study by **Childline**, the service set up for children in distress, reports that **six out of ten teenagers have been asked for sexual pictures or videos**. If this has happened to you, your first reaction might have been to be upset and angry, or maybe you felt flattered that a boy fancied you enough to ask you.

Let's stop and just examine what's happening here when you're asked for a sexy photo or video of you performing a sexual act. What are *you* are getting out of this experience? Nothing.

You are doing the pleasing. You are, in essence, becoming a porn star. You are being used. You are being treated like an object for the entertainment of others. You are living your private life out in public.

Sending a sexy video is not like sharing a passionate kiss where both of you are experiencing pleasure. It may give you a thrill but there is no intimacy. The other downside is that you face humiliation and embarrassment if the video gets out.

It can be hard to know the difference between real affection and when we're being taken advantage of. When we are teenagers, we want to be seen as attractive and grown up. Most of us like to be liked, and any sexual attention we get can seem exciting. These feelings are not bad feelings. They are natural. You just have to be wise about how to protect yourself from being used.

Don't be too trusting. Never make excuses for a boy's bad attitude towards you. Keep your standards high. You are worth it. If you fancy a boy, take some time to get to know him. Work out if you really like him. It is easy to think that if you do not sext or have sex with him straight away (bear in mind, the legal age is sixteen!), he will go off you, dump you, and move on.

If he is this shallow and pathetic, you do not want to be with him anyway. Don't be influenced by what others do or say. You must decide what *you* want to do and what you do not. Don't be a sheep. Be your own fabulous self.

It's true that boys are made differently to girls. They think differently about sex. Boys are more focused on having sex. They are driven by the male hormone, testosterone. Girls, when they fancy a boy, are more likely to fall for the whole person. A girl is normally after a full-on relationship with affection and commitment that down the line may lead to a sexual relationship, while boys always want sex as soon as possible. They are not emotional about it. I am not saying that boys do not fall in love. Of course they do. I am saying that they can have sex and not be in love or even care that much about the girl they are having sex with.

I am not saying this to excuse boys behaving badly. I am just trying to explain that there are differences between us. Knowing this helps you understand boys more, and I hope it helps you protect yourself from some heartbreak.

You are not a porn star. You are a fabulous young girl, soon to be woman, who deserves to be treated with respect. Don't be tricked into believing that you have to have sex to hang on to a boy. That never works. If a boy likes you, he will stay, whatever you decide. If he wants you only for sex, he may have sex and dump you. If you refuse, he may dump you anyway. I would see that as a lucky escape!

On the whole, boys with raging hormones can make life fun. Flirting is all part of school and growing up. It teaches us how to interact with each other. Banter of this sort, when it's not done to hurt or humiliate, can be fun. Everyone gives as good as they get and no one is harmed. But the sexual humiliation of girls that is being learned and copied from music lyrics and porn is very different. This is what many experts are finding can be so damaging.

Any behaviour by boys that leaves you feeling bad about yourself, hurt, or makes you feel inferior to them, is wrong.

You should feel completely comfortable in a teenage relationship. You should not feel you have no option but to do what a boyfriend asks just to fit in. You shouldn't be frightened of being teased and bullied if you don't have sex, or sext, or whatever. No girl should be under that sort of pressure. If you are, you do have to be strong and stand up for yourself and make it very plain to a boy that you are not willing to be treated that way. Do not let him think he can control you by threatening to spread rumours about you or posting nasty things on social media. If he treats you like that, dump him. Now, that's empowerment!

Your feelings are important. You always have the right to protect yourself from any harm, either physical or emotional. If you suffer in silence, it allows boys to think that you are happy to be treated as a sex object.

I want you to be well equipped to make good decisions about who you let into your life and who you have relationships with. I want you to come through puberty strong and wise and with your self-esteem intact. I don't want you to feel frightened of boys or sex, but I do want you to think about what sort of relationships you want and work out how you want to be treated.

For example, does your boyfriend:

- **Get angry when you don't drop everything for him?**
- **Criticise the way you look or dress?**
- **Stop you from seeing friends or from talking to any other boys?**
- **Want you to give up something you love doing, like a sport or out-of-school activity?**
- **Threaten you or call you nasty things?**
- **Hit you or act like he is going to hit you?**
- **Try to force you to go further sexually than you want to?**
- **Frighten you?**

If you can answer yes to *any one* of these things, you are not in a good relationship. Dump him.

Signs you are in a good relationship:

- **You have space to see your friends and do any activities you enjoy doing.**
- **He trusts you and you trust him.**
- **He cheers you up when you are feeling low and goes out of his way to make you happy.**
- **You can talk about anything.**
- **He never forces you to go further sexually than you want to.**
- **He respects you and makes you feel good about yourself.**
- **He shares your dreams and supports you.**
- **He is proud of you when you do well at school and is never jealous of your success.**

six

Sexting

Let's talk about the phenomena of sexting. Sexting is the sending of sexual messages or explicit photos by mobile phone or other device. It's also sometimes referred to as "sending a nudie."

Sexting is simply a new way to objectify and easily humiliate young people. However, it's girls who are at more risk, as they are asked to sext much more than boys are.

Some people argue that sexting is just part of our modern culture. Others say that it is up to the girls to agree or not and that they should be allowed to express their sexuality freely. Some will even argue that sexting can be liberating. This last one would make me laugh out loud if it wasn't so ridiculous and sexist. Aside from the fact that legally, a person has to be eighteen to be shown in a sexual image, it's a one-sided argument and doesn't take into account how emotionally damaging it can be.

It's been a few years since the American teenager Jessica Logan killed herself following the online publication of sexts she had sent in confidence to her then boyfriend. She was so humiliated that she took her own life at eighteen. There have been other suicides too. This is desperately sad. Anything that puts young people through so much mental torture and severe emotional harassment that they think the only way to deal with the shame is to end their lives is bad.

There is no grey area here. Sexting may seem exciting, but it leads to heartache and humiliation.

For those people who have self-harmed or committed suicide after having their naked pictures shared on the Internet, it certainly was not liberating or empowering. It was the opposite.

Sexting is something adults struggle to cope with. For a young person with no experience of sex and relationships or how cruel and judgemental people can be, it can be devastating.

Sexting is happening in secondary schools and even in some primary schools. If these pictures were being asked for by grown men from girls under eighteen, police action would be taken. It would be seen, quite rightly, as child abuse. The fact that sexts are being requested by boys your own age does not make it any less damaging or abusive. You are still left open to the same type of humiliation.

According to the NSPCC's report, sexting is seen as the norm now among many young people. But sexting is illegal. By sending an explicit image, a young person is producing and distributing child abuse images and risks being prosecuted, even if the picture is taken and shared with their permission.

As ever, I want you to think this through for yourself. Let's start with the basic questions. **What does sending a sext do for you?** Maybe it gives you a thrill? Perhaps it makes you feel wanted and grown-up? Perhaps the boy or your boyfriend has promised not to show the picture to anyone else. Well, the sad fact is, he probably will. The temptation not to boast to his mates about what he got you to do will be overwhelming. Even if he doesn't show anyone while you are going out together, if you break up, he may do a spot of "revenge porn." This is posting your pictures online for the world to see, and once they're on there, they're on for life! So the answer to my question, what does sending a sext do for you? Nothing at all.

What does the boy get out of your sexts? Well, obviously, he gets a sexual thrill. But worryingly, more than that, he has power over you because you did what he wanted, and he has practically permanent material that he can use against you for the rest of your lives.

As I've said, he will probably show his mates your private pictures or video. He will then become some sort of hero among the boys who are impressed he got you to do it. However, while his reputation soars, sadly, yours will suffer. You may get bullied and called names like "slag" and "slut." This is totally wrong. It's hypocritical because so often girls are led to believe it's a cool thing to do and that all young people do it. The boy however is not humiliated. It's totally, one-sided and sexist. It shouldn't be this way, but unfortunately, this is the reality of what can happen. It's likely and understandable that you may feel used, ashamed, and embarrassed— because you *were* used. Those are horrible feelings that no one wants to go through. It is even more distressing when you realise that **once something is on the Internet, it is there for life.**

What other harm can sexting do? Well, your sexts can also be used to blackmail you. A boy, or someone who gets hold of the sext, may try to get you to do other things by threatening to show everyone the pictures if you refuse. I don't need to tell you how distressing this could be.

The argument that if you don't send a sext, you will be nagged, bullied, or called names isn't a good enough reason to do it. **In fact, you face the same abuse, or worse, after you've done it.**

As I keep saying, what you do is ultimately *your choice.* You have the right to stand up for yourself and say no. All the way through history, bad things have happened because people were too frightened to say no or to try to stop them. It wasn't until someone stood up and said that slavery was wrong and it should be made illegal that people stopped to think and the law was changed. It was not until the suffragettes stood up and demanded votes for women that we were actually allowed to vote. What I mean is that until girls and boys and men and women are brave enough to speak out against something, it is often seen as normal and therefore OK to do.

As girls, we should not be ashamed of fancying boys and wanting to be fancied. Flirting is fun. There is nothing wrong with that. You should not be ashamed of your body either. What you choose to do with a boy should be personal, private, and special. Sexting is *not* empowering for girls because it puts boys in control. It turns sex into a threat. It takes the fun out of a relationship and brings in fear—the fear of being humiliated and the fear of your intimate, personal photos being shared with everyone on the planet.

Sexting is thought of as part of modern culture by many today. It's interesting, then, that the NSPCC's survey on sexting revealed that boys think that if you sext, you are a slut. Not exactly charming, is it? It proves that deep down, even boys know it's not really OK.

One year-eight girl quoted in the report said: "If a girl went and done this stuff to—dirty stuff to a boy they will get called a slag or a sket if the boy tells. But if a boy does it all the boys think that's cool because they have done stuff."

This comment proves that girls come off worst when it comes to sexting. It's horrible and sexist. It shouldn't be this way, but it is.

As part of the NSPCC report, a year-ten boy told researchers girls who sent sexts had no self respect. He said he would never ask a girl he was friends with to send a sext. When asked why, he said: "Because they respect themselves." When asked if he thought girls that did send them did not respect themselves, he said "They can't be respecting themselves if they are taking pictures of their body and whatever naked." When asked why the double standard, he couldn't explain it.

To me, it also says that boys do not see the pressure they put on girls to sext as wrong. They don't see themselves at fault; they see the girls as the ones at fault. Boys demand these pictures because they can get away with it. It's up to you to show them they can't get away with it.

The more boys think of girls in this way, the worse they will treat girls in all areas of life, such as the workplace. This is dangerous because it turns girls into second-class citizens.

Girls in the NSPCC report also said they didn't always want to sext but were bombarded with so many constant demands, they just gave in. Never give in! You were not put on this planet to do whatever boys say. You have a mind of your own. You are equal to them. Do not put up with this behaviour. No matter how hard it is, you must tell someone if this is happening to you and get it stopped. Worrying in secret is very bad for you. Be brave, speak up, and ask for help. **Call Childline on 0800 1111 if you feel you cannot talk to family or teachers.**

I know you would probably rather roll in broken glass (PS, this is my attempt at humour! Do not try this. It is dangerous and painful!) than speak to your mum or dad about this sort of thing, but please get over the embarrassment and just tell someone you trust. I don't want you to become another statistic of the young people who have taken their own lives over sexting.

We all make mistakes in life, and every problem can be sorted out. Problems are never so big when they're out in the open and shared. You and other girls in school are still children, and you can't be expected to solve all your problems alone. There're not many adults who would find this sort of situation easy to cope with, so don't think you are weak for struggling to cope with such things.

Here in the United Kingdom, **ChildLine** reported that they had received, on average, one call every day about sexting in the past year. Sexting is so common among teenagers that it is described in a ChildLine survey of thirteen-to-eighteen-year-olds as "mundane."

- **Some 60 per cent of children said that they had been asked for a sexual video or photo of themselves.**

- **40 per cent had gone as far as actually creating the content, and a quarter had sent it on to either a partner, a peer, or—in 15 per cent of the cases—a total stranger.**

Disaster! Why would you send this stuff to someone you don't even know? If a total stranger asked you to strip off in the middle of the street as you were walking to school, would you? No. If a boyfriend asked you to get your kit off in a coffee shop or in a busy park or in front of his mates, would you? No. So why sext? It's almost the same. One difference is, you are not there to see them looking at you; the other is that a sext is a permanent record!

Boys don't always seem to pressure you into doing something. They can be charming too. They may tell you that you are beautiful or that they love you. They will use all sorts of pretty words to manipulate you. "But I love you," "You would if you loved me," "My last girlfriend did it," "Having sex (or sexting) will make us closer," and "Don't you trust me?" are all phrases that boys regularly trot out to girls to get you to do something they want but that you may not want to do. If a boy cares about you, he will wait for sex, and if he pressures you into sexting even by saying nice things, he does not care about you. By doing something you don't want to, you are giving boys power over you and your body. You are being treated badly, and you deserve a lot better.

Having a boyfriend should make you happy. It should be fun. It should never bring fear, worry, and misery into your life.

My simple advice is, **never do anything on social media that you would not want everyone, including your parents, to read or see. This also includes your future employers!**

There are just two final things I want to say about this:

Never allow a boy or boyfriend (or anyone) to take pictures of you naked or of your naked body parts.

Never send anyone a "selfie" picture of you naked, even on services that promise to dissolve or erase the message in seconds or minutes once it is viewed. This so-called "safe" service where you can sext might not be a safe as you think. We all know it only takes a second to copy a screen image, and then it exists forever and can be sent and shared with anyone and everyone. My advice is: *don't take the risk*!

seven

Grooming

When I say "grooming," I am not talking about the kind that makes horses nice and shiny. I am, sadly, talking about men grooming girls for sex with them and other men. This is a big problem, and it's happening up and down the country.

We all want to meet someone who really cares about us as much as we do about them. I don't think any girl or woman would say she wants a boyfriend who uses, hurts, and abuses her. But even the guys who look perfect may not be.

Groomers are particularly nasty people who are able to make you believe they do love and care for you when they don't. They want to use you and ultimately make money out of you. I want you to know how to deal with situations like this and to be able to spot the signs of when you are being groomed and manipulated.

How do you know someone really cares about you? Well, that's pretty easy, as I have already said they should never make you feel frightened or humiliated, and they never hit or hurt you. They should never make you do things you don't want to. They should never pass you around like an object and make you have sex with their friends or other men.

A good relationship is one where you respect each other, where there is affection, kindness, and laughter—there is never fear or violence or pressure. I know I have already talked about this to some degree, but grooming is a bit different, and it's not always so easy to realise when you are being manipulated.

Cases of young girls being "groomed" by gangs of men are on the up. Put simply, grooming is the abuse of girls (and boys), normally by older men who seem so sophisticated, funny, kind, and nice that they easily win your trust. They can be charming, and it's easy to think you are dating "Mr Wonderful." After all, when someone is buying you nice things and saying nice things to you and taking you to nice places, it's difficult to think he could be a bad person or may have an ulterior motive for being so nice.

Groomers can strike anywhere. You may be hanging out with your friends at a shopping centre or park or just walking down the street. It can happen anywhere, really, where they can strike up casual conversation. They will start chatting and make you laugh and compliment you. You will like them. They will make sure you do. It's a situation that's so easy to fall into. One minute you're chatting; the next, they know your name, where you live, and your phone number.

Never give out your address or phone number in these sorts of circumstances. Better still, don't strike up a conversation with strange men in the first place. Don't fall for their flattery. If they're older than you, that should send alarm bells ringing. No older man should ever want to go out with a schoolgirl.

Groomers use all sorts of tricks to get you to relax with them and fall in love with them. A common one is for them to ask you lots of questions about you and your family. They are not interested in hearing the details of your life because they care about you. They just want to make you feel that they care. By asking lots of questions, they are also building up a picture of your life that they can use to manipulate you and make you do things for them in the future.

At first, these men make you feel cherished, cared for, and grown up. They treat you like a woman. These are all tricks that the groomers use to get young girls to trust them. It often works. After all, it's instilled in us from a young age to want to be swept off our feet by a man and bought nice things. Remember Prince Charming in the story "Cinderella"? A handsome prince comes along and sweeps a poor girl off her feet and marries her. His motives were good, but life is not a storybook, and sadly, a groomer's motives are not good at all. At first, he will pretend to be Prince Charming, but you will soon find out the truth.

As teenage girls, we often crave to be treated as grown up because we *feel* more grown up than we are. Our bodies are changing, we are attracted to boys, and they are attracted to us. That's normal. What we're not prepared for is to be manipulated. When we're young, we are automatically trusting—too trusting. It's not your fault for being sucked in. It's the groomer's manipulative nature that's the problem.

Groomers often seem much nicer than the boys your own age because they act like they are really interested in you. They are very cunning. They target young teenage girls who have no experience of life, love, and relationships on purpose because they know that young girls have no idea what it means to be groomed. They know these girls will easily fall for their flattery. They also believe that teenage girls are too young to know what a good relationship looks like compared to a bad one. Sadly, in many cases, they are right.

These men mess with your affections and your mind. But you can be prepared. These people tend to follow a similar pattern, as I've said. A man begins chatting to a young girl and gets her phone number and address. He tells her she's gorgeous, showers her with gifts, takes her out in a nice car, treats her well, and makes her think he's her boyfriend and that the relationship is serious. Then, just as easily as you can flick a light switch, everything changes. The groomer changes. He wants something in return. Usually, he wants sex, which girls who think they are loved and in a real relationship are often happy to go along with, even if they are under the legal age to have sex. It is the cruellest abuse of a girl who has no experience of the grim realities of life.

It's when you feel you are in a loving relationship that these abusive men then persuade you to sleep with their friends. This is *not* what happens in good relationships.

The groomers may give you drink or drugs so you don't know what you're doing or where you are. If you refuse to sleep with their "friends," you can end up getting hit. They sometimes threaten to hurt your family, mum and dad, brother or sister. The groomer may have alienated you from your family so that you feel you cannot go to them for help. This can leave you feeling alone and helpless to stop the abuse. This is a very familiar pattern in cases of so-called grooming. This can be the start of a cycle of abuse that can be hard to escape from. You may think that no one can help you. There is always help out there, but it's easier to avoid getting into a bad situation in the first place.

If you find yourself or someone you know in this type of situation, you must tell your parents or the police. If you are too frightened to do that, you can call the free and confidential children's helpline, **Childline**, on 0800 1111. You can also visit childline.org.uk.

I'm not writing about this to scare you. I'm writing this because I want you to know that people like this exist. I want you to know how to spot if you are being groomed. I want you to be wise to it. **Knowledge is power.** In these cases, it is the power to keep you safe.

This whole scenario may seem far-fetched and scary. However, it's a horrible reality, and police regularly deal with these cases. You may have seen them reported in the news.

You may think this could never happen to you (and I hope it won't), but it can happen to any girl. It doesn't matter what your background is. You may have a very settled family life; you may not. Either way, if you're not aware of the telltale signs, you could become a victim, and I don't want that to happen. An older, sexy "boyfriend" may seem exciting, but girls, be on your guard.

I hope that by knowing all this, you can be ready to protect yourself and not allow yourself to get sucked in by these seemingly very charming men who then turn into very dangerous abusers.

I want you to see the best in people, but I also want you to be able to spot the worst and keep yourself safe.

eight
Respect and Self-Esteem

We need to understand that there is no formula as to how women should lead their lives. That is why we must respect the choices that each woman makes for herself and her family. Every woman deserves the chance to realise her God-given potential.
—Hillary Clinton

So, what is self-respect? It's having pride in what you do with your life. It's about being able to stand tall and feel proud of ourselves just because we are who we are.

And what is self-esteem? Well, I think it's the added feeling that you believe you *are* worth good things. It's about believing that you *deserve* happiness. It's about believing that you have a value in society.

Self-respect and self-esteem are vital if we are going to live in society and feel equal to those around us. If we don't have these things, we can feel like the underdog and, as a result, will be unable to thrive and do well.

Having self-respect and good self-esteem is about knowing how you want to be treated and how to treat others. It's being brave enough to sometimes stand apart from the crowd to achieve that. It's about choosing to think for yourself rather than mindlessly copy what everyone else around you is doing. It's about making your own decisions based on what's right for you.

It's a well-known fact that if you don't have respect for yourself, no one else will have respect for you either. If we don't like ourselves or think very much of ourselves, how can we expect others to? If we show others we value ourselves and that we deserve to be treated well, we will be.

Self-esteem is fragile when you're a teenager. For teenage girls, it's easily knocked out of us. If someone is nasty to us or we fail at lessons or exams, we can easily feel we're not good enough. We can start to feel that we don't have a value in society, that we are worthless. That's not true. You are a unique person. There is no other person on the planet like you. Your DNA proves that. What *is* true is that you will feel this way sometimes—we all do. Having good self-esteem allows us to be resilient and to bounce back from such negative feelings.

Good self-esteem shouldn't make us boastful or think things should always go our way. It enables us to cope with failure and learn from it.

> *Take criticism seriously, but not personally. If there is truth or merit in the criticism, try to learn from it. Otherwise, let it roll right off you.*
> *—Hillary Clinton*

Never think you know it all. We never do. No matter how old we get, there's always something to learn. But equally, don't get crushed by criticism. If you think the criticism is accurate, fine—do something about it. If not, ignore it and don't let it drag you down.

If you have good self-esteem and self-respect, the decisions you make are much better than those of someone who doesn't. What I mean is that you will have the confidence to say no to people who ask you to do things you don't want to do or could harm you. You will also have the confidence to accept new opportunities such as a work-experience placement, maybe a new responsibility at school, or even the lead role in the school play! All these things take you out of your usual comfort zone in a positive way. This is a good thing.

Low self-esteem and low self-respect mean that you think negatively about yourself. If this is the case, you are much more likely to turn down new opportunities that could be good for you because you doubt your ability to do them well. Worrying about failing or feeling inferior to others holds you back in life. It makes you less able to achieve success and to deal with the problems life brings. It may even influence the type of people you attract.

Low self-esteem and a lack of self-respect can also lead to you feeling depressed. According to the charity **Youngminds**, eighty thousand children and young people are seriously depressed. About 8,700 five-to-ten-year-olds are seriously depressed, and sixty-two thousand children aged eleven to sixteen are seriously depressed. Online bullying and the breakdown of the family unit are causing this, as well as worries about:

- **Sexting**

- **What others think about you**

- **Getting good grades in exams**

- **Problems at home**

As a child, you can't stop your parents arguing or breaking up. You can't stop your parents losing a job or help them out with money. Stop worrying about what you can't change, and change what you can. Determine to be a success. Embrace your talents.

The importance of self-respect and self-esteem can't be underestimated. They make you strong enough to succeed and strong enough to cope with problems.

Remember, just because you fail at something, *you* are not a failure. Keep trying. You will get better. You are only a failure if you do not try.

Work on getting "sparkle," and keep going forward. It's easy to give up when things are tough. It's not always easy to pick yourself back up, but it is worth it. Refuse to give up. If you give up, you are giving up on yourself and your future.

Girls often find it more difficult than boys to get and hold on to their self-esteem and self-respect. We view ourselves more negatively. It's not surprising when you think about the many mixed messages society sends out to girls or when you consider some of the things we have discussed so far in this book.

Magazines, social media, the music industry, TV, and adverts all tend to show girls in a very sexualised ways. We can't get away from these views because they're all around us. You're encouraged to be sexy and grow up quickly, but when you do, you're often attacked for it and called horrible names like "whore" and "slut." It's no wonder then that it can be a struggle to build up self-respect and self-esteem.

People are impressed when a man stands up for himself or achieves his goals because we have been conditioned over many years to believe that it's acceptable and normal for men to be strong and assertive. He's thought of as macho if he goes and gets what he wants from life. Women, on the other hand, are supposed to smile and be nice. We're not meant to rock the boat or demand a place in a boardroom. We're not meant to be ambitious go-getters. We're conditioned to be caring, sexy and quiet.

Years ago, it wasn't thought seemly for a woman to have any views of her own. She was expected to think what her husband thought or what her father thought. In other words, she was told what to think. She did what men told her to do. She was discouraged from knowing her own mind and making her own decisions. Women fought back against that and proved that they were strong and had minds of their own. But now, it seems some of those old ideas are creeping back into society. Don't let it diminish the person you want to be. Don't let it affect you.

Women face harsh criticism all the way through their lives. There're so many mixed messages out there, double standards, and hypocrisy. Only by examining the worst experiences women go through can you understand why having self-respect and self-esteem are so important. They protect you from not getting consumed and dragged down by these negative and mixed messages.

Having self-respect helps you decide for yourself how you want to be. It means you can see the madness of what's going on around you without falling victim to it. It enables you to see how sexist society is and yet refuse to be stereotyped and hurt by it.

Often, the reason we lack self-esteem is that we are busy comparing ourselves to others and worrying about how we should look to fit in. Forget that. You can never be another person, because you are you. Successful people don't think like this. If you're too busy worrying about someone else, you're not concentrating on you and your achievements. This doesn't mean you can't admire someone for what they have achieved. It just means you shouldn't spend all your time wishing you were that person. Why do you want to be like anyone else? You are fabulous as you are.

Sex and all the issues around it can seriously affect self-esteem. An extreme but good example of this principle in action can be found in the issue of prostitution.

Prostitutes are people, mainly women, who are paid to have sex with men. It's not illegal to be a prostitute. What is illegal is other people making money out of a person being a prostitute or forcing them into prostitution.

The whole issue of prostitution is highly controversial. Some people argue that a woman should be free to choose to be a prostitute if she wants to. Others say that the women are victims and should be helped out of a life that can be damaging and abusive.

As I have said all along in this book, I am totally in favour of women making their own informed choices and being in control of their bodies. What strikes me is that ***prostitution is not a choice if a woman has no other choice.***

Most women who become prostitutes don't think it's a great career choice. The truth is, most women would never choose it as a job. There are many reasons that women become prostitutes. Poverty, a lack of education, and drug and alcohol addiction are the main reasons. These are all things that crush self-esteem and self-respect.

Some women are trafficked into prostitution. Trafficking is a crime in which girls and young women are brought to the United Kingdom from abroad by criminal gangs to be used for sex. Gang leaders tell women who are looking for a better life that they'll get good jobs in their new country. When the girls get here, the job doesn't exist, and they are forced to work as prostitutes. Their passports are taken away, and they have no means of escape. The money they earn goes to the gangs. This is not empowering for the women. It's disempowering. It's also a serious crime.

The fact that much of the media in recent times has decided to call prostitutes "sex workers" rather than "prostitutes" seems almost to sanitise the situation. It makes providing sex to a paying customer sound like a job you could find at a job centre! It hides the often murky truth that many of the women working as prostitutes face. It's easy to forget that these women often face violence and emotional abuse on a daily basis and that the men who make money out of them are criminals.

Some people argue that being a prostitute can be empowering for a woman. If that was true, surely it wouldn't be considered such a terrible and hurtful insult to be called a whore or be accused of dressing like a prostitute. These are words that are used to damage a woman's self-esteem and self-respect. These words are not used to celebrate and make a woman feel empowered and good about herself.

The way people often talk about prostitutes as if they are dirty and worthless sends out very dangerous and negative messages about women. It tells me that women are not being treated fairly in society. It also tells us that there's a lot of hypocrisy around women and sex, and this can destroy our self-esteem and self-respect.

Society shouldn't demonise women for being prostitutes. Society should recognise the damaging effects it can have on a woman's self-esteem and self-respect. It should help to provide another way to live and a way out so that women are never trapped. It's worth noting that the people making big money out of prostitution are mainly men, not the women themselves. This again tells me it is *not* an empowering job for a woman. It also tells me why there is no rush to help women out of the so-called "profession."

I'm using prostitution purely as an example of how women's self-esteem and self-respect can take a battering. I'm not for one minute saying that you will ever have anything to do with this dark and dangerous industry. I just want you to be aware of the deep-seated sexist and hypocritical views that exist in society about women and how these can knock our self-esteem and self-respect.

Sexist behaviour and revolting views about girls and women, no matter what their jobs are, are not going to disappear overnight. I hope that knowing about these issues will make you stronger and more able to push against them.

Self-respect and self-esteem give you the ability to refuse to accept being treated badly and to live your life the way you really want to—and feel happy doing it.

Girls, you *always* deserve respect, and you should *never* feel second-rate, just as you always should respect others and never treat them as inferior either.

Womankind is given a tough time. If you can see why and how, hopefully, that means it won't hold you back.

If you want to check if you're making the right choice about something or that you have good self-esteem and self-respect, just think about how you feel. Does what you are doing make you proud and make you feel happy and confident? If so, you have probably made the right decision. If it makes you feel sad, worthless, or unhappy, then you might want to think again!

nine

The F Word: Feminism

I'm a feminist because I believe in women...It's a heavy word, feminism, but it's not one I think we should run from. I'm proud to be a feminist.
—**Sheryl Sandberg, businesswoman, COO of Facebook, activist, and author of Lean In.**

I have mentioned feminism, but now I want to explore it more.

Feminism is, sadly, a dirty word for many people, even some women, who think of feminists as an angry, man-hating bunch of women who wear boys' clothes and refuse to look feminine. Bizarrely, if you proudly admit you're a feminist, it's often assumed you're a lesbian. A woman's sexuality doesn't even come into it. It doesn't matter if you are male, gay, or heterosexual. You can still be a feminist.

I think it's odd to think that any girl wouldn't be a feminist. It's like saying, "I don't want to stand up for my rights. I agree that I am second-rate to boys. They are superior, and they can make all my decisions for me. They can hurt me and make me feel bad about myself, and I will just put up with it because that's the natural order of things." I hope by now, after reading most of this book, you are angry that anyone could think that. But there are too many people who *do* think like this. That's why we need feminism.

I agree that feminism is a word some girls are afraid of. Some women recoil from the word so much that although they believe in the principles of feminism, they won't actually call themselves feminists because the word itself has been assigned so much prejudice.

We need to take the fear out of feminism.

Feminism isn't just a word that belongs to women. It belongs to everyone who agrees that women are equal to men and should be treated with fairness and have the same opportunities as men. I don't see what's wrong with that. Do you?

It may surprise you to know that men can be feminists and that some men belong to feminist groups. Feminism doesn't mean hating men. It's for anyone who hates to see women treated as second best, unfairly, and only as sexual objects.

Feminism doesn't mean you never want to be paid a genuine compliment by a man or have a door held open for you or to be helped with heavy bags. It means that you want to be treated as an equal and as someone who has feelings. After all, when a man opens a door for you, it doesn't mean you can't do it for yourself. Of course you can. It just means he's being respectful and helpful. I hold doors open for men too. It's polite.

I don't have any time for people who say things like: "Women wanted equality, so get over the fact that a man won't get up to give you his seat on the bus or won't bother to help you carry something." That's nonsense.

Feminism, to me, is about being respectful, and these things are just respectful behaviour. If a man got on a bus or train and was older, or clearly struggling to stand, I would get up and let him have my seat. I hope he would do the same if I clearly looked like I needed to sit down more than he did.

Feminism means fairness in the workplace. It means being paid the same money for doing the same job as a man. It means that as girls, you should have exactly the same freedoms as men. It means not standing for being treated as second best. It means making society know that your viewpoint on issues is just as important and valid as any boy's.

Feminism means not being shouted down as a "crazy" or "bossy" woman when you have a point to put across on an issue. It means not being called a "bitch" just because you had to make a tough decision about something.

At long last, feminism seems to be having a makeover and is slowly becoming cool again. It's attracting young, fresh voices who are waking up to the fact that girls are being treated badly.

More than a hundred years ago, the suffragettes of the early 1900s were jailed, and some even died fighting, just for the chance for women to vote in general elections here in the United Kingdom. Voting was something that, before their brave actions, only men had been allowed to do. At the time, it was widely thought that if women were allowed to vote:

- **Women would be corrupted by politics and that chivalry (old-fashioned behaviour of men towards women) would die out**

- **Women would stop marrying, having children, and the human race would die out**

- **Women were emotional creatures and incapable of making a sound political decision**

Believe it or not, this is what men thought at the time, as indeed did many women. For women to be told these things nowadays would be laughable. After all, we are still here. The human race didn't die out!

These women were the first feminists. They proved that you *can* change things if you're prepared to make a noise about them and not just accept them.

Today, our voices should be highlighting the fact that girls are again increasingly seen only as sex objects by their male peers rather than human beings in their own right. That girls are only being valued for their looks and not their brains. That boys are almost considered to be naturally "in charge of" girls.

Be honest. If they were to walk into a doctor's office, for example, and there were two people there, a man and a woman, they would assume that the man was the doctor and the woman, the nurse or receptionist (many girls or women would too!) We need to change these sexist assumptions.

We need feminism to re-educate boys. We need feminism to show them that lyrics about women in many rap, hip hop, and rock songs that talk about women and girls as if they are dirt are not acceptable. We need feminism to tell them that the images of women seen in porn and in some music videos dehumanise us. Feminism is needed because girls have to show boys another way, not just to make life better for girls, but boys too. I found this on Pinterest.

> *We are not feminists because we hate men.*
> *We are feminists because we respect and*
> *love men and we don't understand why*
> *they do not always return that respect.*
> —*Germaine Greer, feminist, author, academic*

We need feminism because too many girls are growing up where being called a "bitch" and "whore" by boys is the norm. Because being groped at school is being seen as a fact of life. Because our self-esteem and self-respect is taking a battering. Because even out on the streets, young girls in school uniform are being catcalled and propositioned by men. We need feminism because girls need to know what sex really is and what a healthy and good relationship looks like.

Girls, we need feminism because boys and society are labelling girls more and more. They are splitting them into "sexy" girls and girls who respect themselves. There's a subconscious attitude that some girls are tarts and deserve to be treated badly because of how they look or behave and that girls who look more demure are good. These are dangerous labels. All girls deserve respect and to be treated well. Feminism isn't about what you wear. You shouldn't be treated differently just because you are wearing either "conservative" clothes or a miniskirt.

Sex education is not being taught in many schools. This is putting all young people at a disadvantage. Figures from the Health Protection Agency show that **girls are six times more likely to suffer sexually transmitted infections (STIs) than boys**. We need feminism because you have a right to know how these diseases are contracted and a right to know about how to protect yourself from them. Girls, you should not be kept in the dark about the facts surrounding sex and relationships when they can put your health at risk.

Health Protection Agency figures show that out of 15,342 youngsters diagnosed with STIs between 2009 and 2011, 10,439 had chlamydia. This infection can cause infertility in girls if left untreated. Can you imagine having the chance of being able to have children taken away from you just because of a lack of education?

The legal age to have sex is sixteen, as I have already said, but more underage children are having sex, some as young as twelve. I had barely packed away my childhood toys by the age of twelve, let alone was I ready to have sex or even understand properly what it was. Despite the fact that it's illegal, I don't believe that any child feels ready to have sex at age twelve. We need feminism because the oversexualisation of girls means that many are being led to believe that having sex very early is normal. In fact, it's routine (and quite right) for children under thirteen who are found to have had sex to be treated as victims of sexual abuse.

We need feminism because many girls who have sex at young ages, way below the age of legal consent, don't even really know what they are doing. This sounds unbelievable, doesn't it? How can you have sex and not know you are having sex? But it can and does happen. One underage girl, when asked by a police officer if she was sexually active said: "No, I just lie there." It sounds like a line from a comedy, but the tragedy is, this was real. It was said in all seriousness by a child who had no idea what was really happening to her. This is sad. This girl was being abused and was in no way ready for a sexual relationship.

Here are some good websites that give you reliable information about sex:

fpa.org.uk
brook.org.uk

Or you can call:

Sexual Health Line
Free confidential information and advice on sexual health.
Helpline: 0300 123 7123

Terrence Higgins Trust
Information, support, and advice on HIV and sexual health.
Helpline: 0808 802 1221, Monday through to Friday, 10 a.m.–8 p.m.
www.tht.org.uk
You can also e-mail your questions to THT.

Worth Talking About, nhs.co.uk/worthtalkingabout/Pages/sex-worth-talking-about.aspx
Advice on contraception, sexual health, and relationships.
Helpline: 0300 123 29 30, Monday through to Friday, 2 p.m.–8 p.m., Saturday and Sunday, 2 p.m.–4 p.m.

To find out more about feminist campaigns, go to:

ukfeminista.org.uk

We need feminism because too often, we hear people say that if a woman is raped or sexually assaulted while drunk or wearing a short skirt, she was "asking for it." This is nonsense. How anyone can think this, is horrifying. I'm not suggesting that getting drunk is a great thing to do. The legal age to drink alcohol is eighteen. Being drunk or taking anything that leaves you not knowing where you are or what you are doing makes you very vulnerable. Going out and partying is fun. Unfortunately, there are always people waiting to take advantage. The bottom line is, you do have a responsibility for yourself and your safety, but no woman asks to be raped.

Rape and any sexual violence is about hate, sexual control, power over someone, and the humiliation of a person. It's never the victim's fault. The rapist is the one committing the crime. It's not a crime to dress or look a certain way. It's not a crime to trust someone. It *is* a crime to rape someone. I can't think of any other crime where the victim rather than the offender is blamed for the crime.

We need feminism because it's the offenders' attitude towards women that should be put under the spotlight and punished, not the victims.

If a man rapes a woman who was drunk, the woman's reputation is often torn to shreds in court. Some people think that if a woman was drunk or out late partying when the attack happened, then what did she expect? There is the implication that because she was drunk, she is somehow to blame. There is not enough outrage towards the man who took advantage of a woman whom he knew was drunk and totally incapable but who raped her anyway. What kind of man does that?

So here is the quick way of working out if you're a feminist. Put your hand in your pants. A) Do you have a vagina? and B) Do you want to be in charge of it? If you said "yes" to both, then congratulations! You're a feminist.
—Caitlin Moran, writer and feminist

We need to be feminists because the message that is creeping back into the world, thanks to things like easily available online porn, sexist music lyrics, and the whole new trend of sexting, is that a boy's sexuality should dominate a girl's. There is an element of menace coming into sex, and that's not good for women.

Women love sex just as much as men. We should not have to pretend we don't to be considered "good girls" nor should we have to sext to prove we are sexy or cool. We are sexual. We are NOT objects.

We need feminism because we need to have one loud voice sticking up for women. We need to ensure that sexual attacks or violence are never thought of as the girl's fault or excusable. We need to stop allowing society to blame women for these crimes. Putting the blame on women crushes girls' self-esteem and confidence. It makes us feel that we should be ashamed of our sexuality and our femininity. We are who we are. We should not be ashamed of being female. We should not be told to cover up *or* take our clothes off. How we look should be up to us.

We need feminism because girls' feelings are being devalued by society. We are always being told what's best for us. "Don't work if you have children. You must go back to work after you have children. You should only work part time after having children." We should be able to make our own choices and not have society make us feel bad about them. Society should support us in having choices and not condemn us for the ones we make.

We need feminism because we need to loudly tell the world that we are not weak; we are strong and capable.

If women years ago had not spoken out, we would still not be able to vote. We would not be able to work in certain industries such as the police or the armed forces. Single women would not be allowed to get mortgages or buy their own homes without a man's consent. In many cases, women used to have to leave their jobs when they got married, giving up their career and their independence and be kept by their husbands. These are just a few things that strong women who had the courage to demand better for themselves and their fellow women have managed to change by standing up and making their voices heard. They highlighted the unfairness of our society. Not only that, they won their battles, and they made our lives a heck of a lot better as a result.

We need feminism because there's more to be achieved. We need to stop sexism becoming 'normalised' in society.

To be honest, I don't care what you call it—feminism, women's liberation, equality for women, or just fairness. The fact is, women's voices mustn't just be heard, they must be listened to.

What you think and what you feel and the unfairness that exists in our society all need to be talked about and shared. It's the only way that inequalities between boys and girls will be stamped out and the country will become a fairer and better place for you, your mothers, your sisters, and your daughters.

Women's rights are human rights and human rights are women's rights, once and for all.
—Hillary Clinton

ten

Good-Bye and Good Luck

Everything I have talked about in this book is meant to make you feel strong, informed, and fabulous. Right now, you should be tingling with excitement about your future. As young as you are, I hope that in some small way this book has started you down a big, exciting path to finding out the sort of woman you want to grow up to be, what you want from life, and how you are going to get it.

Don't dwell on what your life is like right now or the fact that you have so much work ahead to get to where you would like to be. Don't dwell on the fact that the world is unfair. Just take every day a step at a time. Whenever you doubt yourself or struggle to believe that you can achieve your dreams, get on the Internet and look up the stories of the strong, successful women I have quoted in this book and the many others that are out there.

Research the struggles of the suffragettes and find out about their battle for equality. It's incredible to think of women all those years ago being so passionate about women's rights that they were prepared to die for the cause. It inspires us all to know that those women achieved great things despite the animosity towards them.

There will be days when you feel the world is against you and nothing seems to go right. They happen to everyone. But you have to pick yourself back up. Put on some music you love. Read or watch something inspirational or go and do something that makes you happy. Just get yourself back on track. We all have down days. The difference between those people who achieve and those who fail is that those who achieve do not stay down for long.

I want you to automatically think, "I *can* do that" and not "I can't." I hope that by now, you are involved in out-of-school activities that will stretch your mind and give you new, good experiences. I hope you're excited and driven about the sort of life you want to build. I hope you're excited about the relationships you will have and wise to the ones you don't want to have.

The good things in this world exist for each and every one of us. Whether we are born rich or poor, we are all just flesh and blood. We have the same brains and potential as each other. It's easy to think that doing well is only for the people who are already rich or that men will always have the upper hand when it comes to getting the top jobs. That's not the case. Some of the most successful women came from the poorest of backgrounds or at least very ordinary backgrounds.

Girls, you must not apologise for being female, for having boobs *and* a brain. Your voice and what you say is just as important as any boy's. I hope that by now, you also realise that you don't have to follow the crowd and that you are your own person.

As I keep saying, you have the ability to be and do anything you want to. You are still at school, and your whole life is ahead of you. From your little desk at school, you can learn enough to take you anywhere you want to be in this world.

Not every day will be easy, and this puts a lot of us off going for what we really want from life. It's easy to think, "Why should I bother working hard when everyone else is out having fun?" If you're good at what you do, there will always be opportunities.

There is a wise proverb: **"Do not love sleep or you will grow poor; stay awake and you will have food to spare."** Basically, this means don't slob about—get up and get on with it!

Remember, you don't get to become a great sportsperson, doctor, artist, musician, actress, hairdresser, businesswoman, politician, engineer, computer whizz, forensic science officer, or whatever you want to be without hard work, some self-sacrifice, and single-minded determination.

When nothing is going right, just remember that what looks impossible *can* be achieved if you want it enough. Sometimes you may just have to tackle it a different way, or push yourself that bit harder.

How many times have great sportsmen and women fought back from a losing position to win a match? "Lots of times," is the answer. Great tennis players pull a match back from the brink of defeat all the time. When you think the odds are stacked against you, remember that.

I'm sure you've heard adults say things like: "I always wanted to be a fashion designer but ended up selling clothes instead. I don't know how, time just ran away from me and I was too busy having fun. I wish I'd given it a go." That's a regret. Regrets have a nasty habit of gnawing away at us in later life and making us thoroughly miserable, and in some cases, even depressed. Even if today has been rubbish for you, there is always tomorrow.

As Scarlett O'Hara says in one of my favourite books, *Gone With the Wind*, "Tomorrow is another day."

It is. And every day you get up is a new start. You can make some incredible things happen if you try.

As I have tried to point out in this book, some of the biggest names in fashion, sport, business, music, and politics came from very humble beginnings. Remember, everything is possible if you want it enough. The most successful people believe that, and you must too.

It's not easier for one person to achieve things than another. It's just that people who do make it refuse to give up, no matter what. They have this incredible drive and determination, and that is what you need to have too.

> *Life is not easy for any of us. But what of that? We must have perseverance and above all confidence in ourselves. We must believe that we are gifted for something and that this thing must be attained.*
> *—Marie Curie, 1867–1934*

Marie Curie was a physicist, chemist, and pioneer in the study of radiation. Her work was crucial in the development of X-rays in surgery. She was awarded the Nobel Prize in Physics. (Google her. She's amazing!)

It's great to achieve your dreams. Don't forget, though, that the route to getting where you want to be is fun too, and the experiences you have along the way will give you some of the best memories of your life, memories you will talk about in old age.

You know I am passionate about you getting a great education because that allows you to get a good job and gain independence. It brings security and freedom. These are two things that women in many parts of the world can only dream of. So be ambitious and determined, not just for you, but for them too. Show the world what women can achieve if they are allowed to. Democracy and freedom are things we are used to having here in the United Kingdom and in the whole Western world. Don't take them for granted. They're precious.

When I think about the countries where getting an education can get girls killed or abducted, I feel an enormous pride that we have a free education system and that our society wants girls to be educated. How can we help those who are not so lucky? Well, we can do it just by achieving our goals and speaking up for our rights.

In Nigeria, extremist groups are kidnapping schoolgirls and selling them. Male-run extremist groups in some countries want what they call "Western" education outlawed. Education does not belong to a culture. It belongs to humankind. It's a right of each and every one of us, no matter what our colour or religion. Education makes our world a better place. It breeds tolerance and sparks invention. It allows us to question and invent.

Some of the world's greatest philosophers and teachers came from non-Western countries. They were educated to the highest level, and it's so sad to see young girls in those same countries being denied the chance to learn too. After all, it's education and equality that make a country strong. Without education and equality, a civilised society can't exist.

In countries where education isn't free and there are no government benefits, children jump at the chance to go to school. They know that education is their only way out of poverty and a route to a better life. In places like India and Africa, children often walk miles to go to school. Here, where school is compulsory and free, it's seen by too many as boring.

You may not be very academically oriented. I was never destined to be a professor of maths. But school gives us the chance to try out all sorts of things and find out what we are good at. Grab your chance to learn and try out new things. We should appreciate all that we have for the sake of those girls who would jump at the chance of getting a good education.

It's sad to say that it's often only when something is taken away from us that we realise how good it was. Don't let your schooldays pass without getting as much as you can out of them.

Poverty entails fear and stress and some-
times depression. It meets a thousand petty
humiliations and hardships. Climbing
out of poverty by your own efforts—that is
something on which to pride yourself, but
poverty itself is romanticised by fools.
—J. K. Rowling, multimillionaire author
(most famously of the Harry Potter series)

JK Rowling has amassed a fortune from her worldwide best selling books. She was a single parent struggling for money when she was writing her first Harry Potter book. She now works with many charities to help children and single parents. Her story is remarkable. It is one of incredible acheivement and it is an inspiration to everyone who has a dream.

Some of you reading this are already studying hard to make your dreams come true. You may have access to extra tuition, good schooling, and supportive parents. But many of you don't. If you don't already have a lot of opportunity, it doesn't mean you can't succeed. Even if you don't have a clear, burning ambition yet and you think that passing exams is pointless, you *will* be good at something. Your job is to find out what.

I am aware that life is not peachy for everyone reading this. It may be difficult to find somewhere quiet to study and do your homework or even work out what you want to do for a career. Talk to your mum or dad or a teacher. Really think about what you want from life and go and get it. Be proud to be a strong and independent girl, and don't be frightened of hard work or standing out from the crowd. It will make you an incredible and successful woman. It's so tempting, but don't get so engrossed in social media that you fail to stay in touch with the outside world. There is so much more to do than that. You are the next generation of artists, doctors, musicians, businesswomen, politicians, and scientists, or whatever you want!

I found this and wanted to share it with you:

If a child lives with hostility she learns to fight.
If a child lives with ridicule she learns to be shy.
If a child lives with shame she learns to feel guilty.
If a child lives with tolerance she learns to be patient.
If a child lives with encouragement she learns confidence.
If a child lives with praise she learns to appreciate.
If a child lives with fairness she learns justice.
If a child lives with security she learns to have faith.
If a child lives with approval she learns to like herself.
If a child lives with acceptance and friendship she learns to find love in the world.

—Anonymous

My point here is that it's important to know how vital the way we are treated is to building our character.

You are *fabulous*. Truly believe it! Be different and dare to make your dreams come true.

Printed in Great Britain
by Amazon